FROM THE LAND AND BACK

FROM THE LAND AND BACK

CURTIS K. STADTFELD

DRAWINGS BY

FRANKLIN McMAHON

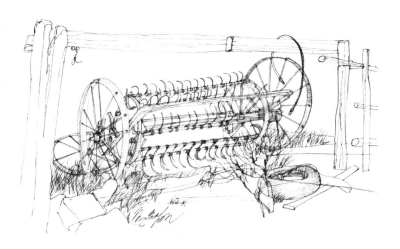

CHARLES SCRIBNER'S SONS · NEW YORK

Library of Congress Catalog Card Number 76-38946
SBN 684-12944-2

FOR MY FATHER

CONTENTS

FOREWORD
by *RENÉ DUBOS*

It is now fashionable to explain human behavior by the survival of traits originating from prehistoric life. According to this view, man's tendency to become part of a gang—whether in the street or in a corporation—and his propensity to kill are modern manifestations of Stone Age life. However, *From the Land and Back* reminds us that life on the farm encouraged the development of qualities far different from those which make for a successful hunter; it suggests that much of modern life is the expression in a contemporary context of human traits which emerged when primitive man became a farmer.

For the longest part of man's existence, it is true, he obtained sustenance by hunting wild animals and by gathering nuts, roots, and other plant products. The primitive hunter-gatherer way of life lasted so long—several hundred thousand years—that it has certainly left an indelible stamp on the biological and behavioral characteristics of *Homo sapiens*. But this does not mean that human nature has been shaped only by that pattern of life. The biology and psychology of modern man have certainly been influenced by the fact that many more people have lived on the earth since the end of the Old Stone Age than had during the hundreds of millennia before. Most of these people, furthermore, have lived in man-made environments, eating food produced through their own toil rather than derived from the wilderness.

All over the world, population density increased explosively as soon as the supplies of food became more abundant and more dependable as a result of the domestication of plants and animals during Neolithic times. Of the 80 billion people who lived on earth during the past 100,000 years, 70 billion have lived since the first agricultural revolution which occurred approximately 10,000 years ago. The hunter's exciting life still survives in our collective dreams because it is part of our very distant biological past, but the austerity of the peasant's life is also part of our heritage and has provided the disciplined atmosphere which enabled man to colonize the earth.

Large settlements began to develop shortly after the agricultural revolution, and there have been huge cities ever since the Bronze Age. But in any period, up to modern times, the immense majority of people lived on farms or in small villages. All cities, furthermore, have been largely populated by immigrants from farming areas, and they continue to depend for their survival and for their growth on a constant transfusion of new blood from the countryside and from impoverished lands. To a large extent, the attributes which make for success in the city are still the traditional peasant virtues. Men have not yet reached the stage of a truly independent urban civilization, and they may never reach it. It would be surprising if the agricultural ways of life, which have conditioned the existence of more than 80 percent of the human beings who have ever lived on earth, had not made a lasting impact on man's nature, probably as much as and perhaps even more than the hunter-gatherer ways of life. The modern world is occasionally the expression of man the hunter, but man the farmer governs most aspects of daily existence.

Life on the farm has of course continuously changed with time and in particular has progressively become adapted to different climatic and soil conditions. Until recently, however, it retained some of the essential characteristics it acquired at its very beginnings, during the Neolithic and Bronze ages. Practically all the species of animals and plants used in agriculture today were first domesticated thousands of years ago by the primitive farmers. Many agricultural practices are also of very ancient origin and continue to rely on the use of equipment fundamentally simple in concept; the plow is still based on the design first invented by the early Egyptians, and not until the Middle Ages did windmills and watermills began to supplement human and animal labor. Until now, most farmers have lived close to the land in small social groups rarely exceeding 500 persons and almost out of contact with the outside world. They have had to develop a high level of self-sufficiency and independence and to learn how to operate within a narrow range of social contacts. Limited as they were, the ways of life imposed by agriculture were not without rewards.

FOREWORD

They provided the farmer with a place of his own, where he could be fairly comfortable, do work of which he could be proud, achieve relative security, and derive stability from the depth of his roots in the soil. In *From the Land and Back* Curtis K. Stadtfeld has given an enticing picture of traditional farm life. This was a world in which, as he states, huge barns were built with immense care largely out of pride, an attitude which monopolized much of the farmer's energy because it was one of his chief sources of satisfaction.

After retaining their essential characteristics for thousands of years, the agricultural ways of life began to change profoundly and abruptly a few decades ago, especially after the two world wars. As the song has it, it proved difficult to keep the boys on the farm after they had seen Paree. Social contacts were vastly enlarged by more rapid means of communication, by the great variety of mass media, and, of course, by the much increased social mobility. Industrial wealth created new expectations and demands. Most important probably was the fact that scientific technology made possible entirely new methods of agricultural production which resulted in higher yields through the use of improved plant and animal strains, of fertilizers and pesticides, and especially of sophisticated equipment powered by electric or internal combustion engines.

Farming, which had been largely a family enterprise in which even young children played an essential role, suddenly evolved into a highly specialized and capitalized industry. The New England Puritan and the early Middle West settler regarded farm and family as part of an integrated social structure through which man controlled nature and exploited it under God's guidance. In contrast, the corporate farmer or rancher in Texas or California is as likely to live in a town house as on the land. He uses high-powered equipment and immense amounts of chemicals to convert natural resources and forces into money—practicing the same kind of cold efficiency he would apply to the management of an industrial operation. He has hardly any more sensual and emotional contact with soil, animals, and plants than an engineer in an oil refinery has with the crude petroleum and distilled products. Just as the engineer buys the gasoline for his car at any convenient place, unrelated to the refinery where he works, so does the manager of the corporate farm buy his food at any convenient supermarket instead of maintaining a garden. The more industrialized the farms become and the more oriented to a money economy based on the efficient production of a few products, the more financially profitable they are likely to be. But this kind of success is often achieved at the cost of an impoverished life for the farmer, providing him with little emotional satisfaction.

Curtis K. Stadtfeld's book marks a dramatic moment in the history of mankind. He describes in detail the kind of farming which has lasted for 10,000 years as an individual enterprise, then reports almost with puzzlement the sudden change to farming conceived as a corporation. The present styles of corporate farming, based on scientific technology, have certainly not yet reached their final form. They are bound to evolve with further scientific knowledge and under the pressure of economic and ecologic constraints.

FOREWORD

But, barring massive social upheavals, there is little chance of going back to the individual, familial pattern of farming so precisely and lovingly described in *From the Land and Back*. It would be false and useless sentimentality, indeed, to hope that a longing for the past could revive a form of agricultural enterprise incompatible with present economic and social conditions. But it may be useful to identify the human values which made the family farm play such a large role in the development of civilization for a hundred centuries. For, to repeat it once more, most of human life during the past ten thousand years has been spent on small family farms.

As mentioned earlier and richly illustrated by Mr. Stadtfeld, life on the family farm usually implied a high level of self-sufficiency. The farmer could not survive, let alone make a profit, without some measure of competence in the management of soils, waters, and woods; of animals, plants, and machinery; of social contacts and market conditions. General farming was the opposite of narrow specialization.

The breadth of experiences associated with life on the family farm was of special importance for the development of children. From his very early years, the child was exposed to an immense variety of stimuli—the rich spectrum of colors, sounds, scents, forms, and temperatures associated with the changing moods of the hours, the days, and the seasons—as well as with the diversity of artifacts and occupations required by farming activities and self-sufficient life. The modern city child can also be exposed to a wide range of experiences, in the form of books, pictures, displays, radio and television programs, trips to the country and to the seashore, but this kind of experience is qualitatively different from that of the child on the small family farm. Most of the urban child's contacts with the outside world are passive; he behaves as a spectator, not necessarily out of choice, but because society does not allow him to intervene in its operations. In contrast, the child raised on the family farm could hardly avoid responding actively, almost as a young animal, to the natural events around him; furthermore, he was expected to participate usefully in the work of his family and group; he was responsible for certain chores. In the modern city, the child has hardly any notion of what his father is up to when he leaves for work in the morning, whereas the child on the family farm had to share in his father's activities. One need not be a professional psychologist to know that the experience of the passive spectator is by no means as enriching and creative as that of the person who participates actively in the event. Information hardly ever becomes formative until it involves active participation.

Recent studies of the origins of American scientists have revealed that a large percentage of them emerged from small colleges of the rural heartland Middle West. Surprising as it may seem, the famous universities of the East Coast have been proportionately less productive of distinguished scientists.

Another social environment which has yielded a large percentage of people distinguished in many aspects of American life—including science—is the Lower East Side of New York City. Although nothing could seem more different from the family farm than New York's Lower East Side, in fact both social situations had certain aspects

FOREWORD

in common. At the turn of the century, the streets of the Lower East Side displayed the multifarious skills and trades of the immigrants, with the immense and picturesque variety of their products and talents. The children of the immigrants grew in a wonderfully diversified world and futhermore were expected to participate in most of their parents' occupational activities. Social ambition of course played a large part in all East Side success stories, but there is no doubt that the diversity of environment and the opportunity for active participation created an atmosphere in which each child had a chance to discover himself and to develop his potentialities.

The proletariat of the Lower East Side has evolved into a stolid bourgeoisie, and farming is rapidly becoming industrialized. It would be folly to try to revert to the past. But it is wise to remember that the small family farms and the East Side pushcarts contributed an immense wealth to American life—a wealth derived from the rich diversity of surroundings and from the opportunities they offered. To children, in particular, they provided an immense field for concrete experiences and for active participation in exciting activities.

At the end of the book, Mr. Stadtfeld has left the farm and, with his wife and children, now lives in the city. As he explains, the title, *From the Land and Back*, does not necessarily mean a return to the kind of farm life he had known in his youth, but rather to the richness and diversity of experiences which provided him with the material for his haunting and rewarding evocation of a moment in the history of man.

INTRODUCTION

This is not simply a work of nostalgia, although some of that has gnawed at me for nearly twenty years and now I think it is in perspective. On the one hand, this is the story of my farming forefathers, of how they picked a somewhat inhospitable portion of central Michigan, put their roots down, made farms and homes and futures, and how all that they built for generations was swept away almost overnight by technological change. It went so fast they hardly knew it was gone. Such change is sad, for it uproots people of long standing, destroys subcultures, and leaves the children without roots.

So this is also the story of how a generation found itself thrown out of its homes because the homes had their foundations cut away. There are many better books to tell how those young people, now parents themselves, are afraid that they have lost their own lives and perhaps lost their children at the same time.

But this book tells, besides, of what it was really like to live on the land. At its best, it was a life of great enrichment and fulfillment, a life whole and organic and satisfying.

INTRODUCTION

Much of the time, it was a life of boredom and compromise, of brutal work and disappointment, of the harsh realities of poor medicine and indifferent nature.

And, I have tried to show how fragile a rural society is when it is based on isolation and ignorance of the outside world. That is a lesson that those disenchanted young people who seek the simple life of the farm should know. They should know, too, that it is not in nature to support man very well. We have always struggled against nature, tried to make ourselves more comfortable, more secure. A few years ago, we thought we had finally conquered nature. Now we see that there may be a finality about it more profound than we had anticipated.

For every step that man makes in rising above nature is at the expense of something else. The moment we killed an animal to eat and wrapped ourselves in its skin while we made a fire we started the process of upsetting the balance of nature. We are learning that we must strike a bargain with the environment: so much comfort for so much imbalance. We know now that we can take out too much, just as you can whip a horse too hard.

It would be nice if those of us who find ourselves confused by urban living and think it would be better to go back to the land could remember exactly how it was. This is an attempt to remember.

I know that men remember things they have forgotten. There is a stirring in us for real fires, for something in us recalls when it was a real fire, not an automatic furnace in the basement, that kept us warm. There is an urge to hunt, a wish to garden even if it is no more than trimming the lawn. There is a deep instinct to protect our property, and there is a lure to the land. The memory is locked away in our minds that, somehow, it made more sense when we grew our food for ourselves.

But to argue that growing our own food is more natural is to beg the question. There are too many of us to go back to the farms, even if we wanted too. And our historic struggle is away from the farm and the forest to the city. We must learn how to live in the cities, for that is where our future lies, if it is anywhere.

Some of my friends have questioned the title of the book, saying that they understood my feeling of coming "from the land" but wondered whether the title means that I intend to go "back." My reply is that I never came away from the land, any more than any of us ever comes fully away from the physical and spiritual experiences of our childhood. I once thought I had come away, had become fully urbanized, and people who know me well have been surprised to discover my rural roots. But I did not come away spiritually, and I now go back, not in a physical sense but in a recognition, which I hope is a mature one, of how important this life was to me and to many of us. None of us can go back in time or space, but if we are lucky, we can use the things we learned to help us understand what we have become and why.

I hope this story is moving now and then. I hope that it is sometimes funny. Most of all, though, I hope that it is true.

FROM THE LAND
AND BACK

1. THE HOME PLACE

Our hands were lighter on the land then. In central Michigan a hundred years ago, the lines laid down by nature still held for the most part. Time and the glacier, winds and rains, had scraped and pushed and silted the soil into short hills and narrow valleys, into rich rolling expanses not quite broad enough to be plains, into lakes and swamps and here and there oddly barren little spills of bleak soil pinched in between gravel pits and marl bogs. The trapping was about as good as ever, which wasn't very much, but the deer were plentiful. The Indians had never taken the country very seriously, and they were pretty shrewd judges of quality in such matters.

Other parts of the state were more enticing to ravishment. A little to the north, the great white pine forests marched to the horizon and in the last decades of the nineteenth century greedy lumber barons were busily ravaging that resource. The lusty lumberjacks left behind them legends, most of them made up from sheer boredom and the poverty of reality. More importantly, they left behind great vulgar cut-over areas where only stumps and rotting tops and underbrush remained; a kind of early-stage, low-grade Nagasaki, a quality of destruction not yet much advanced by technology. We had only begun to learn about the pillage of nature, and the battle was still on fairly even grounds.

Nature had anticipated man, or at least destruction, and had built restoration schemes into her system. Jackpines popped up when the shade of the mighty whites was gone, and the scrub trees and the Kirtland's warbler began the job of reforesting, while native ferns and quack grass held the land in place. Although man had destroyed a product, he had not destroyed the producer and nature moved to reclaim the land and start over. The deer came back out of the swamps and grazed in the clearings.

The lumber companies were not through, however. They had land to dump and mounted campaigns to sell it cheap to farmers. And where they had seen a quick profit, settlers saw something more lasting—a chance to live and develop and improve, a chance to have their own place.

For many who came to settle there were a few short years of hope followed by disillusionment. The thin layer of fertile topsoil built by the pine needles vanished so quickly that many drifted away from their farms before the land was fully cleared. There is an untold saga of crushed hopes and spirits haunting those short-lived farms, and it is remembered in huge tumbledown barns in desolate areas where the land would not support the dreams. Some of those big barns were never filled with hay, and some only once or twice with boughten hay hauled in to feed the horses used by the lumbermen. Most of them are falling in on themselves now or are already gone. Few were ever painted; in a little while none of them will be left standing.

Besides the long-trunked pines, there were white birch and poplar, trees that nature kept for her own uses. The birch is a lovely but brittle tree. Indians, and later small boys, made canoes from the bark, but this minor value was about all that could be extracted from the tree. A few determined souls developed recipes to boil parts of it for food, but only for fun or in desperation. Later, men learned to harvest the scraggly pine and poplar for pulpwood to feed the paper mills, but these were, first and finally, quick-growing scrub trees designed to aid reforestation after forest fires or logging.

The topsoil was light and thin, sandy stuff that could be converted to the uses of agriculture only with skill or in special circumstances. Along the lovely coast of Lake

FROM THE LAND AND BACK

Michigan, moderating breezes carried in a climate ideal for the cultivation of fruit trees, especially red cherries. For the Indians, it had been a land of legend, where sand dunes became mythical sleeping bears. White men found the Grand Traverse Bay area one of those bonuses of nature, a place for the growing of good things, a special haven in Michigan as the Napa Valley is in California. Near towns and, later, cities, dairy farms were profitable. With careful attention and the technical skills that were developed years later, potatoes could be grown. As railroads poked around the state, the shipping of butter, grain, potatoes, and cattle became profitable.

The slice of eastern Mecosta County settled by my ancestors enjoyed few gifts of nature. The climate was tolerable but hardly encouraging. The quality of the soil could not match the farmland of the great plains, built by centuries of grass and extending into the lower tier of counties in southern Michigan. Farther east, the rich flatlands of the state's "thumb" region were cordial to sugar beets and beans.

But Mecosta County is a grab-bag mixture of sharp, eroded hills and small rich flatlands; of blowing sand and dark loam; of swamp and rock, pine and oak, sumac and white clover, often all on the same quarter section. My people chose this land partly because it was cheap at a few dollars an acre. The railroads and lumbermen had promoted it, and the settlements scattered out from the southern and eastern parts of the state, becoming smaller and poorer as they reached upstate.

The community was Roman Catholic. St. Michael's

THE HOME PLACE

church is high on a hill in Wheatland township; the bells in the 90-foot steeple could be heard over most of the parish, and sermons were preached in German. The railroad was half a day distant by team. The lumbermen had come and gone, leaving behind the stumps that still dot the landscape. Farther north, farmers had come and built the big barns and the little houses, and they had drifted away when the barrenness of the land became apparent. My ancestors were more tenacious, or perhaps simply more stubborn, or with fewer alternatives. They put down roots—their own and the roots of crops. They called the farms their places, with perhaps more meaning than they knew, and they stayed. As time drew on a little, sons bought land near their fathers' farms, and the first farm in the family was the home place.

Scattered stands of the great white pines still towered over the trails when they moved in. Sometimes, there had been too few to interest the loggers; some of the trees may not have been quite large enough; sometimes, one suspects, the lumbermen simply became bored with their exploitation and moved on before the cutting was quite complete.

Double-bitted axes and two-man crosscut saws felled those remaining big trees. The tops were hauled together and burned. The trunks were sold as logs or, more often, sawed into boards, planks, and timbers for the houses and barns and sheds. Oxen or horses powered stump-pulling machines to tear out the roots and they were hauled into rows to make the first fences. Some of those stump fences still stand. The tough roots are still strong and tangles of natural growth have made them inpenetrable—hog-tight, we used to call them. Some might resist tanks as successfully as the hedgerows of western Europe. The dense roots gave a quick, intense heat, lighted easily with the old Lucifer matches, and warmed hands and baked pancakes on cold mornings.

It seemed all of a piece . . . the men and the land and the buildings of native pine and stone and the church. An organic unit, all parts surrounding one another and sharing strength. Men found fulfillment in hard work, in hope in the future, and in the church. Youngsters lived a near-ideal life of joy and freedom. The women worked the hardest, sustained by hopes for their family and their faith in God. They had the heaviest burdens, and they needed the land less and the church more. Childbirth was a regular rendezvous with death, illness a flirtation with disaster. Weather, like the soil, was more often than not an enemy. The fertile field, the pleasant day, the rich harvest were occasional gifts to be relished, not commonplace or expected.

In those days of early settlement, it was a quiet land. The muscles of men and beasts cleared the land and reaped the harvests, and a man could hear himself, his neighbor, and quite literally his God as he worked. Compared to the shriek and shatter that signal today's construction projects and progress, this work made only a murmur that barely disturbed the white-tail deer, the red-tailed fox, the gray squirrel or the blue jay, or the woodchucks that watched curiously from the bracken.

The crows stood their ground and cawed a protest against every invasion of their sanctuary. Their calls were among the loudest sounds.

THE HOME PLACE

There were no radios, no airplanes in the sky, no automobiles on what passed for roads. A creaking windmill or a wood saw might be heard a mile away. Bells high in the belfry on the church rang at noon and at six, and their sound carried so well across the parish that, as my father recalls, "we unhitched by the Angelus." Today I hear the chimes from the University bell tower both at my home and at the office. They provide some continuity, but the bells meant more then. A man was pulling the rope, not an electronic device. They were our bells, and they tolled for us.

That stillness had not been completely shattered when I was a boy. On a calm night, we could sometimes hear a neighbor stowing oars on his boat when he finished fishing in a lake half a mile away. We never belled our cows, but we could hear his. A horse's whinny might be heard two farms away. In the summer, we could hear the stones clank against the cultivator on the back 40.

The sounds of our childhood must have a major influence on the sounds we create for our pleasure as we mature. The screaming roar of our cities seems to relate to the din of contemporary rock music; the sounds of my father's childhood were friendly to the waltzes and hymns we all grew up with.

Natural noise is mostly gentle. Tall trees brush each other gently; leaves of shoulder-high corn rattle a little when a boy runs through them. The same corn crackles as it ripens and dries in harvest time. A wheat field bowing and dipping in the wind sighs; summer breezes whisper as they flow around wooden buildings or through the stump fences. Farmers added other sounds—cackling chickens scratching in the dust; cattle lowing, happy to come home from pasture to barn; stamps and snorts of horses eager to be out and about their business; the clatter of harness and the creaking of wooden stanchions strained by cattle reaching for the last licks of hay or oats; the clean ring of a stream of warm milk squirted into the bottom of an empty pail; the long low groan of soil turning under a steel plow; the guttural grunts of pigs, speaking only German.

The first need was subsistence; then a few dollars to buy the things the farm could not produce and to retire the mortgage. By the time my father left the home place to start his own farm, a few years after World War I, the system had been honed to a level of success that made many parts of life richer than they had ever been before, or perhaps since.

Subsistence meant beef and pork, milk and butter, poultry and eggs, vegetables and fruits, all available in generous quantities, even for the eager appetites of big families of farm children.

Horses came next, for the land had to be tilled, and all manner of other work was at hand. Horses had to be bought; few men raised colts. A team would be enough for 40 acres, but a farmer with 80 needed at least three horses, and a quarter section (160 acres) required five or six. Two horses drew a single-moldboard, 10-inch walking plow, and could cover an acre a day. A slightly larger riding plow took three horses. Not many farmers used the larger hitches in that region; a four- or six-horse combination took too much room to turn and move. Most of the fields were better suited to two- or three-horse unit. More prosperous farmers, or those with more vanity, might keep a special horse for a buggy or even a light team for trips to town. It was not unusual for a farmer on 160 acres to own seven or eight horses. Their feed—hay mostly, but some oats too—required upward of 20 acres.

As for cattle, it seemed logical to have a breed that served two purposes—milk and meat. The farmers called them Durhams, though they probably did not know that the cattle were so named from the county in northern England where they were first bred. They were descendants of oxen but bred to give more milk and to fatten well. Registry standards were developed under the name Shorthorn, and the breed is now known as the dual-purpose Milking Shorthorn, a big-framed animal, with mature cows weighing 1,400 to 1,600 pounds. Nowadays these cows may produce 300 to 400 pounds of butterfat in 8,000 to 10,000 pounds of 4-percent milk. Fifty years ago a herd average of half that much was probably good. Some of the male calves would be steered and fattened, to be sold at two or three years of age weighing 1,200 or 1,500 pounds. Prices varied wildly, but at $3 to $5 a hundred pounds, the steers could make a substantial contribution to cash income.

Those big cattle ate a lot of hay. To support a cow, with the young stock needed to replace her after a productive life of five or six years, the farmer might need 4 or 5 acres of hay and pasture and another acre in corn and oats to provide grain in the winter.

Fairly early, the farmers learned to make corn into silage. The whole corn crop—stalks, unripened ears, and all—was chopped in late summer and blown into a silo. It would partially ferment and be dug out in the winter as a nutritious green feed that put fat on steers and balanced the diets of milk cows. The first silos were built of wooden staves like huge barrels. The acids rotted the wood rather quickly, and as money became available, the silos were rebuilt with concrete staves or poured concrete. A few were made of steel, but the acid attacked steel almost as quickly as wood. Even the concrete had to be replastered every few years. But a 4- or 5-acre field of corn, stored in this way, would fill a 10-by-30-foot silo with 50 or 60 tons of good green feed.

Prosperous farmers, or those developing a dairy specialization, built their silos of glazed tile. These were more expensive, but more durable, and where they remain today they mark a farm where dairy herds once flourished.

Today most silos are of glass-lined steel, sealed to prevent spoilage, highly efficient, and incredibly costly.

A herd of eight or ten cows produced more milk than even the thirstiest family could drink. Farmers formed a cooperative creamery to make the cream into butter. Through the 1940s, the Remus Cooperative Creamery was one of the largest of its kind in the world, making a superior rich yellow butter that went out by the railroad carful to the cities of Michigan and even the East.

The cows were milked by hand until the 1940s. A good hand might milk six or eight; a farmer with two or three boys found his maximum herd size at a dozen or fifteen cows. After both morning and evening milkings, the milk was brought up from the barn to the house in 12-, 14-, or 16-quart pails and run through a cream separator. This hand-cranked centrifuge spun the cream from the milk. Cream was carefully stored in the basement to keep cool for the weekly pickup by the cream truck. The cream check came every second week, a stable income. Prices were nearly as good then as now. In the 1930s, butterfat sold at 50 or 60 cents a pound. A good cow might make a pound a day in full production, so a ten-cow herd might provide an income of $30 or $40 a week, no small sum.

The skimmed milk by-product—it was never called skimmed milk; always simply skim milk—made cottage cheese for the table or for the hens, and the remainder became part of the slop for hogs. It was widely believed in that area that hogs could not be decently fattened without skim milk. It was also believed either that skim milk was the best possible food for calves or that it would kill them. Scientific analysis of this kind of question was not rampant. It would have spoiled many heated arguments across line fences, or before church, or over a pinochle table.

It is a fact, however, that shoats fed on skim milk and a corn-and-oats bran grew quickly into sleek and marketable hogs. Various slops became prized family recipes. Some farmers fed simply skim milk and dry grain; others added potato peels and other ingredients to the milk stored at hog-house temperature in a big barrel and fed to the pigs rather sour. The pigs never seemed to mind; they fattened on whatever was available, using an extraordinary ability to manufacture amino acids as needed and converting virtually anything to fat.

Butchering day was even more than a social event; it came close to being a tribal ritual.

A farmer might select two or three hogs for butchering.

These were usually not prime specimens, but aging sows grown so big they could no longer keep from rolling on their litters and killing them. They might weigh 500 or 600 pounds.

The work began days before. Pine roots were gathered, along with solid logs, for heating water in the scalding troughs and caldrons outdoors. The gallus—a tripod of poles bolted together at the top—was erected over a bare place in the yard. Neighbors were alerted. Butchering was usually a business involving three or four families, which took turnabout to help one another.

The butcher day itself was actually a day and night of long hard work, one of those days when a man feels rich and generous, when special skills came into play, and boys found themselves called to unusual tasks. Fires were lighted early in the morning, and by the time pre-breakfast chores were done, the water should be near boiling. The big victims were dragged to the scene of slaughter, usually screaming and displaying incredible strength. A .22-caliber shot in the brain dispatched the hog; short ropes were tied quickly to the back legs, and the carcass was strung up, head down, heels at the top of the gallus. Sometimes, holes had to be dug to let the head swing free. The throat was slit and the animal allowed to bleed.

Some of the oldtimers used to catch the blood in a large pot. A boy would be assigned to stir it constantly until it cooled; if this were done properly, the blood would not coagulate. It was then made into rich, strong-flavored blood sausage. Later, slaughterhouses were so equipped that the hogs could be strung up by their heels; then their throats were cut and they would bleed to death. This sounds incredibly cruel, but it is crucial to get the blood out of the animal so that it does not taint the meat.

Once the hog was dead, the great carcass was rolled in the boiling water of the scalding trough to soften the coarse hair, which would then be peeled off with scrapers fashioned of dull-toothed pieces of steel fastened in a circle and attached to wooden handles. It was a matter of pride to scald well and scrape clean; one of the forgotten skills that once gave a special satisfaction when done well. The carcass was then hung again on the gallus, disemboweled, the head cut off, and the rest of the body divided. Small parts of the head made delicacies; my mother, at my insistence, once fried the brains for me. I do not recall enjoying the taste, but I had read somewhere that hog brains were delicious and I so exclaimed.

These huge hogs were encased in great layers of fat. Much of it was cut off and dumped into a big old black tub called a rendering pot. This pot was mounted over a fire and the lard was boiled until it was clear, then scooped out, filtered, and stored, to be used for cooking all year around. All these rendering pots were old. Apparently no one ever bought one new.

Bacon was cut in huge slabs, perhaps 10 to 30 pounds each, coated with a curing material (I recall it as having much more flavor than Shake 'n' Bake, although its function was similar), and the slabs were hung in the basement to cure.

If the farmer had a smokehouse, the slabs of bacon, the hams, and all the rest of the meat were hung from poles and treated to long exposure over a smoky fire. The smokehouse would be filled for weeks with the smoke and smell of curing meat; sometimes you might catch a whiff a farm or two away, upwind. The house was about the size of a privy, and the fire was small, devoted to smoke and not heat or flame.

Hog intestines were not dumped or wasted but carefully cleaned and saved to use as sausage casings. Parts of the hog to be made into sausage were cut into small pieces and mixed with seasoning. Usually there was one man in the neighborhood with a reputation as a good sausage maker, and he would be in charge. The intestines, cut into short lengths, were slipped over the outlet spout of a grinder, rolled up as a woman rolls a stocking before putting it on her leg. The grinder, usually clamped to the edge of the table where the mixing took place, would then be turned by a strong man, while others fed the pieces of pork into it. Out the snout the mixture would come, into the intestine, which was then tied off into links. Again curing followed, and the winter's sausage was ready.

The pieces of hide left when the lard had been rendered away were dried and used as a snack called "cracklings"; they enjoy occasional popularity still as a bar snack, now packaged in cellophane, and thinner than in their more rustic state. All boys considered them delicious.

Another forgotten use of pig parts was the tail as a skillet greaser. The tail was cut with a square of rind and fat attached, 4 or 5 inches square and as thick as the lard, and served as a greaser all winter. In the spring, it was thrown out, even if not used up, because by then it would begin to stink.

Recently I heard a woman in a supermarket exclaiming over the insensitivity of friends who had killed a calf they had raised: "Why, I would choke over the steak if I thought, 'Well, I'm eating old Jack.'" Perhaps it was because we did not know better, or perhaps we were simply more brutish, but the pork and bacon, the sausage and ham, tasted better to us in the winter because we knew exactly how they came to be on the table. We would comment: "Andrew sure made a good sausage this time," or "Peter sure did a good smoking job on this ham." It may be too much to say that the food somehow had more character because we were involved in it personally; I know only that there was a closer relationship than there is to the packaged meats we buy in the store.

This closeness had another effect. We grew up with an attitude toward animals entirely different from that of city-raised people. We knew that they were there for our use. We might be fond of a cow, but if she failed to produce, she was shipped to market forthwith. A dog that could not be trained, or that chased chickens, was dispatched, without rancor but without hesitation. Stray dogs and cats might be carrying disease from another barn; they were shot whenever possible.

None of these attitudes caused any reduction in our affection for animals. The family dog enjoyed privileges and status that was probably envied by some wives. One bitter day when my terrier came home and died of accidental poisoning and I was unconsolable, an older brother made a caustic remark, probably in a clumsy attempt to assuage my sadness, and I tried to punch him in the nose. We cared about our cattle and horses and had respect, if not affection, for the pigs.

Some of the sayings of the community centered on the singular behavior of hogs, for instance. One man was fond of saying something like: "If you see a hog, kick it. It's either out, been out, or thinking about getting out." Another favorite descriptive phrase was to say that someone was "as independent as a hog on ice." Curious boys in the city wonder why the swirl that water makes in the bathtub drain is always in the same direction; curious farm boys wonder why all hogs' tails curl the same way.

Obviously the hogs were an important part of farm life; besides providing a variety of meat for year-round use, and fat for cooking, they served a social purpose in bringing neighbors together in a common endeavor.

Chickens served multiple purposes, too. They gave fresh eggs for the table or for sale or trading; they were handy for a quick dinner, for fresh meat in winter, for Sundays and holidays. They ate wheat and oats and barley and corn, shared the table scraps with the pigs, and ate cottage cheese made of skim milk. They always barely managed to escape when the wagon rolled through the yard.

Yet, somehow, pork and chicken do not satisfy a man's soul, if they do his stomach. Pork was called "the working man's meat" in the tacit acknowledgment that it is second choice. It is the beefsteak, the beef roast, the flesh meat of cattle that finally satisfies, that the psychologist calls the "reward food." Skill can raise the flesh of fowls or pigs to great heights of taste. Both are more efficient than cattle in converting crops to flesh; both are quicker to raise, cheaper to acquire, simpler to care for. But man does not name his pigs, except in a perfunctory way if they are registered. He does not pat chickens and seldom talks to them.

With the development of efficiency and automation in recent years, we have happily provided hogs with automatic feeders and left them to fatten alone. We are content to have hens live out their lives in wire cages, laying eggs that roll down gentle inclines and are packaged without ever being touched by human hands. We are not so comfortable about automating dairy farms. The loafing barns and milking parlors have taken away something of the personal relationship between men and cattle and they both miss it. Given a choice, many dairymen would prefer the old stanchions where the cattle could be cleaned and groomed and cared for.

Part of this feeling comes from the fact that chickens and hogs are ultimately hostile to man. A hen seated on her nest is perfectly prepared to peck the hand that feeds her if it tries to reach in and take the eggs which she wants to hatch. If a man bursts suddenly into a hen coop, the flock cries out and runs. Cattle, like horses, will come to you, but a hog cares nothing for you. Now and again one hears a grisly story about a farmer's having a heart attack and falling unconscious into the hog pen; the hogs simply devour him. A cow might lick his face.

City dwellers may know nothing of this consciously; yet the steak house has greater prestige than the chicken-in-the basket operation, and money is only part of the answer. A man wants his friends around him, after all.

The cattle were always more important psychologically than the pigs and chickens. Recently, I came upon the farm record books that my father kept in the 1930s. I kept the one for 1935, for my birth is recorded in it. But as I looked through the books, something appeared that absolutely astonished me. Income from the eggs was often equal to or in excess of the income from the dairy herd. Yet the hens were always somehow regarded as a nuisance, kept by Mother for "pin money" but not really a part of the farm system or the family economy. Our attitudes did not square with reality, and the reason was that the cattle were more companionable.

The horses were even more a part of the family. A few farmers kept on the old teams even after they acquired tractors in the 1940s. They justified the cost and difficulty by saying that there were still jobs that the horses did better. And there were. For picking stone, for loading grain, or in other cases where the horse would start or stop with a voice command, they were much more useful than was the tractor, that strong but ignorant machine which, like a computer, does precisely as directed, no more, no less; while the result is always billed as favorable, the machine can sometimes lead you into trouble. But whatever the excuses, the real reason for keeping on the horses was sentiment. The specter of the glue factory was just too grim; many old horses simply lived out their days at pasture until they either fell dead or became so feeble that they were put away like an old dog. Mercy killing did not require debate.

Stocking of the farms had a profound influence on the entire cropping operation. If a farm had a patch of swamp or woodland that could be used as "permanent pasture," so much the better. Gradually farmers came to realize that this term was often a euphemism for condemning the cattle to slow starvation in the summer. But for many years, it was the accepted method of summer feeding. It persisted until dairy farming and a cash economy came to dominate.

One neighbor owned a large swamp, and his scrawny scrub cattle spent the summer there. We were offended, not because of any particular affection for his cattle, but because it was obviously bad management. My dad used to say scornfully that the poor cows had to search through the swamp for a clump of grass, and then smack their lips over it and hope it would turn green sooner or later so they could have a little something to eat.

When the highway was improved just after World War II, with a good broad base and thick gravel, the contractor bought an odd hump of a hill that stood at the front of that swamp, hard by the road. Shovels scooped away the hill, and the dump trucks hauled it away for filling and broadening. We always suspected the owner made more money from that than from the scraggly cows which had grazed there.

There was something symbolic about that hill's being trucked away. It was one of the first major changes in the landscape wrought deliberately by man in an attempt to improve things. The swamp no longer flooded the road in the spring. The road there was not so steep. And the drive to town was not the same any more. Removing that hill was the first step toward the construction of those enormous interchanges and expressways that cut up the landscape now, putting man's print on the countryside in an indelible way and separating him so sharply from the natural contours of his land.

A year ago, my wife and I drove over the continental divide west of Denver at the Berthold Pass. We left the city on a broad expressway that suddenly, just below the divide, gave way to a steep narrow road that snaked up the side of the mountain and had to be negotiated in second gear with great attention to staying close to the mountain side. We agreed that laws should be passed to prevent the construction of a graded highway over this high point. As long as the climb is still there, a feeling remains of how difficult it was for men and wagons to make the journey in the first place. I recalled the hill gouged out of the swamp, and I wonder, a quarter of a century later, if it should have been done. We may some day learn how to strike a balance between useful progress and the thoughtless gouging away of the land. We are becoming more cautious in these judgments.

Sooner or later a need arose for high-quality pasture for the milk cows, as well as lower quality for the horses and the other stock. The same rule applied to the need for hay; the best is none too good for milk-producing cows, but timothy or other grass is plenty good enough for horses and dry stock.

Small grains—oats and barley and wheat—are needed, not only for the grain. Horses need some oats, chickens require wheat, and the cows could use oats and barley along with corn for the milk-making grain. But also great mows of straw are needed for bedding. Wheat yields the most straw; bright-yellow long straw that looks almost good enough to eat and makes fine bedding. But it irritates horses' skins, and they prefer oat straw. Sometimes dry cornstalks and corn husks were shredded and used for bedding or feed, but they are poor quality for either. Corn fodder—so called no matter how it was used—does not soak up the moisture in manure as well as straw does, and it tends to twist up and clog the beaters in the manure spreader. As feed, it is low in nutrition.

By fall the big barns were full of hay and straw and corn fodder. Hay was hauled loose in those days and piled high in one or two mows. The ponderous thresher was parked on the floor in the center of the barn, and the straw blown into another mow, if possible one from which it could be poked down directly over box stalls or stanchion rows. If the corn fodder was saved, it was blown into still another section, for horse feed and such bedding as it provided. Hogs needed straw, too, and we used it for chickens, although it was not very satisfactory. Later, we learned to use ground corncobs under the chickens. Highly absorbent, they made better bedding than other natural materials.

The need for space to store so much was the reason for the huge barns, but they also came to be measures of the size of the farmer's dreams. They had individual character that expressed their owner, and their state of repair was an index of a man's success and the quality of attention he paid to his work. The barn was more important to the farmer than his house, it received more of his attention, was the focus of more of his thoughts. In that part of the country, there were few fine houses but many great barns.

Today, the need for storage space is only a fifth or even a tenth of what it was then. Much of the winter feed for cattle is stored in silos, where both corn and hay are easily kept and mechanically fed. Hay and straw are baled or chopped. The bales can be stacked almost anywhere, even outside under a waterproof cover or in cheap low sheds which hold many more tons than the high old mows. Many farmers used trench silos, which are just that— trenches dug in the earth. Corn or hay is chopped and dumped into them, then covered with plastic held down by rows of old tires. Spoilage is a little higher than in a regular silo, but the cost of construction is low and the feeding is easily handled.

Thus the big barns were a necessity at first, a redundancy now. They were less economical, but more fun for boys to play in. There was a thrill in raising a big barn; it was a social event, a time when a man put his mark upon his land. And there was a personality, a permanency, about them not found in the present-day pole structures with steel roofs.

Nature is reclaiming the old wooden barns, recycling them. They stand abandoned, like great sailing ships stranded in a world where there is no more wind. They fall in or burn away. The weathered old boards are stolen or bought to sheath houses or panel family rooms where people seek to borrow a mark of endurance from the past. The barns that remain are atavistic relics, victims of change as surely as the decaying tenaments of an inner city. They were built well out of pride, a quality that held a larger share of man's attention in less prosperous times. They were the mark of the man who built them. They were not designed with the tax advantages of accelerated depreciation in mind. They had a spacious elegance about them, and, like the mansions of the rich, they became too expensive to afford. The factory-designed sheds that have succeeded them are more efficient, more economic, but there is no kinship for them, and they have no space for a man's spirit. Progress has diminished the soul for the sake of the pocketbook.

We never played in the chickenhouse. The chickens' care was "woman's work," in the unconsciously sexist phrase of the day, which meant that while the damn things were probably necessary, attending to them was generally beneath a man's dignity. Women, usually more practical than men, were glad to have the chickens for their fresh eggs and fresh meat, and for pin money, and if that meant they had to take care of them so be it.

There were men who made their living in central Michigan in the 1930s and 1940s as seasonal travelers for the poultry business. Their status also reflected our attitude toward the hens. Cattle buyers were highly respected; they drove big trucks and smoked cigars and stopped by the tavern for a drink with the men. But when the poultry dealer came into the area, he talked with the women, and the children, he did his work, and he went on his way without pausing in town. His work had no such prestige as that of the men who dealt in cattle. We admired the stockmen, as a city child might admire the skilled steel workers who build bridges or skyscrapers. But the poultryman was consigned a second place; his urban counterpart might perhaps be a store accountant, one whose work was necessary but hardly the stuff for a boy's dreams. The broker wears the colors of his product, then as now.

At first, hens were simply allowed to sit on eggs and hatch out chicks. But by the time a flock of 100 or 200 or 300 was wanted, it became easier to order the chicks through the mail. They arrived in the spring, cheeping away in cardboard boxes, and were set out in warm corners of the brooder house. This was a special building, on skids instead of a foundation so that it could be pulled from place to place, giving the little chicks new ground to run on each year without exposing them to any diseases the earlier flock might have had.

They grew quickly and in a matter of weeks would be ready for culling. This involved separating the males and females, the former to be sold as little fryers, the latter to grow into hens. The poultry dealer would come by in his pickup truck and we would sort the flocks, catching individuals with a long heavy wire, bent at the end so it would snag a foot and we could pick the chicken up. We would let it dangle upside down until we had determined its sex, then either set it free again or put it into a crate. The crates of fryers went away in the truck for so much a pound.

By fall, the roosterless flocks would begin to lay their sterile eggs, hens laying five or six a week in a frantic futile attempt at self-perpetuation. The men were in charge of setting out the brooder house in the spring and towing it back in the fall, putting up the fence around it while it was in the field, and getting the hens into the coop in the fall; the women and any reluctant children who could be forced to help, filled the feeders, dumped water into the water devices, gathered the eggs, and endured the cackling and senseless running around and pecks on the hand.

Manure from the coop was not abundant, but it was about the best fertilizer we had. It was usually reserved for the garden or for a sandy spot we were trying to build up.

In later years, when specialization began to replace diversification, the chickens were one of the first things to go. This was not necessarily because they were the least profitable part of the farm enterprise; as I have said, those little flocks of laying hens often had an economic importance that is rarely recognized. In any event, record keeping had not reached a stage where the farmer could tell very clearly what was making him money and what was not. The chickens went because no one ever liked them much.

That attitude, economically unrealistic but emotionally satisfying, was the key to much of the organization, the planning, the development of that system of farm life as it existed before and after the turn of the century, and with fairly minor changes until World War II. The farm families had not yet been captured by the technological centrifuge that separates every action and plan in terms of efficiency. They liked red cows or Jerseys depending on their

(27)

background or on their farms, and so they kept those breeds. Today the Holsteins dominate the dairy industry, largely because their milk has less butterfat, more in line with the needs of the market. In short, the farms came to be more industrial, more oriented to a money economy and to efficient production of selective products—specialized as opposed to general farming—they became less whole, more impersonal, generally more profitable, perhaps less satisfying.

Many were glad to have it so. The old way of life was generally relinquished with enthusiasm. It was, at its worst, hard and exacting, brutal and narrowing and depressing. Yet it is part of the perversity of man that in matters of social change he always seems to throw out the baby with the bath water, at least in America. We seem willing to scrap entire systems if they fail at any point. Black people have left the South, hoping that the injustices they suffered there would not follow them north. In fleeing, they were simply following the example of the rest of us, who have always fled—to new land when the old wore out, to new territories when the old began to fill up, to Oregon if New York did not seem fertile enough, always restless, always moving on in hopes of something better. Perhaps we are too idealistic, or perhaps we have simply not been forced to sit down with our problems and solve them where we are.

My ancestors had left Germany hoping for a better life. It is difficult really to grasp the idea of what it was they sought, for their dreams were formed in a time so different from ours that, although we are talking about my great-grandparents, we might as well be talking about people from another planet.

They were spared the effects of mass communication. Knowledge and notions were more durable; their beliefs, both right and wrong, were passed on from generation to generation. About the only advertising they were subjected to was the Sears, Roebuck catalog once a year. And even that was to some extent an endless shopping list, a wish book, rather than a high-powered stimulant to consumer wants.

To realize how simple their wants were, you must imagine how much simpler your own would be if you had no television to acquaint you with idealized versions of how others live; if you had no newspapers or magazines to bring you enticing visions of creature comforts and machines that would do your bidding; if you had no radios to sing the praises of a million useless delights; if you had no movies to bring you brilliant fantasies of glamour and ease; if the news of the day did not provide instant information about events in Moscow and Delhi and New York and Mylai; if you had few books and journals; if your knowledge and awareness of the world were expanded only by infrequent conversations with occasional passersby.

Their vision of the world and the dimensions of their dreams were easily fitted to the boundaries of their parish. They were less confused by facts, since far fewer were available. They were in fact closer to medieval society than to the slick jacked-up oversold world where their grandchildren wander, half lost and confused, in the 1970s.

They had come to the land, they had explored its resources, and in a primitive way they had turned them to their needs. A man could be born and live a full life and die within the limits of his farm. He was not plagued by thoughts of wealth, for he was not reminded every few minutes that others were more wealthy than he. He was not oppressed with the drive to acquire, since the opportunity to acquire was not pressed upon him. And for perhaps half a century he was not spurred with the need to move about, for the space around him was sufficient that his ancestors and his progeny could all be found within walking distance. A man had his place. And he could find solace in the Bible, believing that his place was good. For a little while, as cultures go, he had found the haven that he sought.

That system worked because it gave those men what they wanted, and it was not just because they wanted so little that it worked so well. They wanted precisely what we all want—a place of our own, socially and physically, a place where we can be comfortable, do work that we can be proud of, be with friends and family, share security. Their way of life gave them roots, literally and figuratively. They could see the spot where they were born, the work they did last year, the initials they carved a half-dozen years ago. They knew the ancestors of the cattle they milked and of the families they worshiped with on Sunday. They sank deep roots, that cannot be shaken loose even now by time and change. For they were part of time in a way those of us loosened from the land cannot be, and change was on their side. In cities, where man builds and wrecks, change is normal. On the land, nature's instinct is to conserve, and change is the intruder.

That lasting sense of place was built into the men and women who grew up in the area. The hills and forests wrapped around them, measuring their space and adding to the sense of lasting security. The great plains in the west have no distances, only horizons, like deserts, but in my country the natural lines of nature give lasting form to every farm, and a man can pick his way down a lane in the dark twenty years later.

A recent spring, I walked through my father's fields, and it was as though an unplanned multimedia explosion was taking place in my brain. I had worked and walked these fields for years, and every step or striation evoked a memory, something I had not remembered to forget. Here was where we worked one weekend to dig out that troublesome rock, using shovels and finally dynamite. The soil is a little lighter here now, because we finally gave up and buried the rock. Here is where you needed to shift the old Oliver 60 tractor from third gear to second to make it up the hill with the 7-foot double disk. Here is where you had to shift from fourth to third when hauling a wagon of potatoes from the back 40. Here is where we buried Biff when he came home to die, full of rat poison set out by a careless neighbor. Here is the old fence post where the bluebirds nested every spring. Here is that deceptive soft spot, fed by a tiny underground spring, where I got the manure spreader stuck and hung up two tractors trying to get it out before Dad came home. Here is where a friend ran the tractor into the fence when I let him drive it against my father's orders. This is the rock we converted into a Japanese Zero in the 1940s. Here is where I seeded a watershed of clover to end the steady erosion. That is the post where we used to hang the electric fencer. This is the field where the corn was left out one winter and the deer came and ate it, flocking in by the hungry hundreds, while we stood by, more or less helplessly. Here is the loose rock in the foundation wall of the barn where I used to hide my homemade guns at the end of a day of play. And so on, foot by foot, stone by stone, post by post, tree by tree, an anchor in time and place which no one will raze for a tenement, tear up for an interchange, bulldoze for a subdivision. A place where you can go back and remember what it was like to be ten or sixteen or twenty. Where you can go back, always, and the crows still protest your coming and the deer still hide secretly just behind the cover of the forest.

We were at one with the place, and we were victors over time because we were a part of the cycle of the seasons and there was not a beginning and an end, except in the cemetery we could see from the barn hill. The assembly line has no cycle, except the annual stop for model changeover. An accountant's work has only the cycle of the fiscal year, separated from the changing of the seasons.

Slowly, as we grew up, we became aware of that cycle and we grew into it. At some point, the winter would begin to weaken and the snow begin to leave. The cows would stay out in the barnyard, instead of huddling by the door, anxious to get back in as soon as the gutter was cleaned. The sap would begin to run in the maple trees, and grass begin to green.

Then the welcome hectic life of summer would be upon us. Manure to be hauled, oats to be sown, the ground to be tilled for corn, fences to reapair. By the time the corn had been cultivated once, the cows had become accustomed to summer and it was time to make hay and cut wheat. Oats came a little later; get them in quickly before the weeds came through, to suck up the energy of the soil as soon as the oats stopped pulling on it.

Just a little break then, after the hay and grain are in; cultivate the corn for the last time, walk through the oat stubble and see if the seeding of alfalfa and clover has taken root. It is next year's hay and pasture.

Fill the silo, dig the potatoes, make a second cutting of hay, stuff the barn with everything you can find, race the winter like a squirrel filling his tree hole, like a bear building his winter fat. Can the fruit, do the fall butchering, ship the spring pigs, fat hogs now, patch the cracks in the barn wall, cut wood.

And then the storms would come, and the country would settle in, barns fat with harvest, cows full of milk and young, the soil waiting again under the snow, the cowslips dormant in the swamp, the deer growing hungry in the woods, but your cattle sleek and secure with you against the cold.

A man went through this with the wonder of childhood, when all the times of the year were playtimes, when the spring was a time of little floods when shingles became boats, when the winter made the barn hill a sled slide, when the ice storms meant no school. He went through it next with the exuberance of youth, when he built his muscles and worked without prodding for the sheer joy of it, and later, with his own land and crops and cattle, when it stopped being a game but was a time when a man could do his best and not be counted a failure for any reason but laziness.

And when his sons came along, he could see it all through their eyes, living it all again, watching them learn and work, pray in the same pews, maybe use the same milk pails; knowing that someday he would lie beside his father in the cemetery down the hill from the church and watch smugly from heaven while it went on again and on and on and on.

2. THE LAST GENERATION

The cycle shattered in my parents' generation. A way of life that seemed durable and certain came quickly to confusion. In one lifetime, the old system dissolved, almost vanished, save for a few back corners of the county where old men hang on, ignoring change, sometimes confused, sometimes bitter, pathetic in their passion to cling to the past.

It had seemed so complete, so full, so logical. Only a clairvoyant could have seen how fragile it was. A man had his life and his living in the land and the livestock. There was support for his family, and he could look forward to a life of well-rewarded hard work with a place to give to his children. A woman had her husband to clothe and tend, her children to raise with a security of promise. They could look ahead together, man and wife, to a circle of friends and family, the sustenance of the church, the durability of a way of life where continuity controlled change.

Yet it all toppled, as quickly as a revolution changes a government. Henry Ford found profit in mass production of automobiles, then trucks, and isolation diminished, almost disappeared. The first weak radio signals reached the farms, received on battery-operated radios or crystal sets. It seemed only a moment later that the television tube saturated us all with constant messages from around the world.

The Wright brothers flew, and man broke loose from the bonds of land travel. That first shaky flight, a year before my father was born, evolved in his lifetime to man on the moon. The glitter and promise of money danced in the cities, and the farm children were promised a release from the endless toil in the fields.

No one sensed how complete the revolution would be, nor how it would separate us from our landmarks as it separated us from our burdens. For many, what had looked like promise grew into despair, and that betrayal of promise lies at the root of our bewildered behavior as we struggle to adjust to the new ways. To some, the shock of change was shattering.

All this was out of sight, out of mind, when my parents, with a confidence that must be completely absent in young people now, took their wedding vows. Young people marrying in the 1970s have confidence in themselves, if they are lucky, and in each other, but in little else. But when my parents were married in the 1920s, they could add to that confidence a faith that all the things around them would endure—the way of living, the society, the church, the economy, the family—and that their dreams and hopes would be the dreams and hopes of their children.

The church where they were married stands barely a mile from the house where my father was born, and they bought land and settled halfway between church and birthplace, so close that in the evening after the chores were done they could walk to either place before nightfall.

My mother's family had wandered, from New York to Canada to upstate Michigan and finally to Remus. But wandering was alien then, and the object of wandering was to find a place to settle, to make a home place of your own. She was glad to find a man with roots; her parents were pleased, though they were town people and might have preferred if their new son-in-law had opted to come and be with them. But no more than two miles would separate them. They were close.

He was a big, strong, husky young man, had finished the eighth grade, cut ice for pocket money, knew how to run a threshing machine, to harness a team, to plow and pray. The courtship was a clumsy one, and they told us funny stories about it for years until we were old enough to know the truth.

Mother used to claim that she had seen Dad many times, but that he was a blacksmith, always dirty, and the first time she saw him clean she fell in love with him. He claimed that he had married her on a bet, and that at least had some semblance of truth.

The fact was that she was a schoolteacher, who had gone to Central Michigan College (now University) for a little while, taken a third-degree teaching certificate, and taught in a little wooden building a mile south of the church. The schools were later consolidated, and the building has been gone for years, but it still stood when we were little. Last spring, I drove by on my way somewhere and noticed that there was a crop planted on the spot where the school had stood. But the outline of the school-yard was a darker green, a natural marking recalling a place set off from crops for learning.

Her family had come to Remus and bought a big old barn of a restaurant. They were an old family; the name had originally been Upjohn and they recalled proudly that their present name, Merritt, had been bestowed upon one of their forebears by an English king for some forgotten service. They loved their frail young daughter, slim to thinness, quiet, devoted to duty as defined by her parents, wearing steel-rimmed spectacles, serious.

Dad later told us that when the Merritt family came to Remus, he saw a schoolteacher, a bright young woman, and told his friends that he thought he would just marry her. They courted briefly, and he told her that she must become a Catholic. Her family objected; they had an historical distrust of Rome and Romanism, but she gently overruled them and lived her life in the devout religiosity special to converts.

She had saved a little money and so had he. They moved

into a house that was at once nearly elegant and nearly un-inhabitable. It was a house already with a history, as was the farm they bought from Dad's father.

The house was the successor to a big old gingerbready place, built by a slightly shady operator who had amassed a modest fortune through gambling, politics, speculation in land and timber, and other things since forgotten. The old man had built his house at the front of a 40-acre plot, bought with gambling profits, and used it as a home base for his various activities. While he lay there in his final ill-ness, the house caught fire, and he was carried out to the woodshed to watch it burn. "See," his young wife was said to have told him, "there goes your big house." "Let her go," the dying man replied. "That's the way I got her."

His widow rebuilt, but the builders took advantage of her, and when her money ran out, the upstairs was not fin-ished, the various angles of the roof did not quite meet, and when my parents moved in, it was like a house abandoned, half complete, left behind already.

But it was big. The kitchen was huge even by the stan-dards of those times, when the kitchen was the center of family life. The dining room was as large, and so was the living room. One big bedroom was downstairs, and there were four more upstairs. Tacked onto the back were an entry hall, a big room no one ever had a name for, and still another room that Dad used as a workshop. A wide porch ran all along the front, wrapping around both ends. An aimless house, with cherry trim but pine floors, the duct-work for a furnace but no furnace, two porches besides the front one.

FROM THE LAND AND BACK

Our family devoted years of spare-time work to tearing off parts, knocking it down to a manageable size. The back rooms came off, solving the problem of roofs that didn't match and always leaked. The front porch came off, robbing bats and snakes of a home. We covered some of the floors with hardwood, painted some walls, finished rooms in the upstairs as children needed them for bedrooms.

The house was always cold in the winter. The wood-burning stove in the living room could heat that room, but the upstairs was left to the elements and we slept under all the old blankets we could find. In winter, the frost would form on the inside of the windows up there, building up in severe winter to an inch thick. Urine in the chamber pot would freeze overnight. Mother used to laugh, later, and claim that one winter it was so cold in the house that when one of my brothers, playing on the floor, wet his diapers they had frozen him fast to the floor. Winter baths, taken in galvanized tubs upstairs, were to be avoided. The outside privy was forbidding, and one of the benefits of being a boy was that, in the winter, you could go to the barn, where it was warmer, to answer calls of nature.

Dad and Mother had bought 120 acres of land from Dad's father, bickering with him throughout their lives because it should have been 160. There was the 40 that the house stood on; a 40 behind it, making the conventional long 80, a quarter-mile on the road and a half-mile deep. Another 40 was attached to the back, making an L-shape. Dad always thought he should have had the other 40, which would have given him a square parcel. But his older brother, who bought the home place, refused to give up that piece, because it was in a creek floodplain, rich and level, good potato ground. They both needed it, and Dad lost out, and no one can be sure how much that particular event changed the lives of us all. The conflict between Dad and his brother was never really forgotten, a hostility that put a little space between the families all their lives.

Much of the farm is heavy soil, good for wheat and corn and hay. The back 40 is sand and swamp, too light for conventional growing of demanding crops. Dad tried to grow potatoes on it all his life and never had a really good crop but once, in 1937, when he bought the only new car he ever owned, a 60-horsepower Ford V-8.

Where the soil was right for potatoes, the combination of dairy cattle, hogs, and potatoes made a complementary and profitable mix. While potatoes need loam or light soil to grow best, they also make a heavy drain on fertility. If the soil is made rich with manure and plowed-down sod, it can produce a good crop. Now, of course, extremely heavy applications of chemical fertilizer, irrigation, and technical spraying techniques have moved the balance more in favor of the farmer. But before those methods were developed, careful crop rotation with hay and small grain crops prepared the way for the potatoes. And it did not pollute the creeks.

Besides rich soil, potatoes demanded great quantities of hand labor in harvesting. When the plant matures, the vines above the ground wither. A digger with a big steel point was hauled along the row. The point would be below the depth of the potatoes and would root them up onto a roller which shook them loose from the dirt and dumped them on top of the ground. We picked them from the ground by hand and tossed them gently into wooden crates, each holding a bushel. The crates were gathered onto wagons and the potatoes hauled to the house for sorting.

Many farmhouses had storage space in the basement for the potatoes. They were kept there in the cool dark until the market was right. The smaller ones and those with blemishes were thrown away and the rest bagged for shipping.

The hands for all this work were those of schoolchildren. Grown men, especially those whose middles had thickened through the years, could not do the stooping to pick the potatoes from the ground, although they provided the strength to move the filled crates, which weighed about 60 pounds. It was traditional to have one or two weeks of "potato-digging vacation" from the school. Education would stop while the harvest was brought in. Youngsters who did not live on farms where potatoes were grown hired theselves out to other farmers and picked the potatoes for 5 or 6 cents a bushel. This glut of work came late in the fall, after the corn was in the silo and the grain was harvested. In terms of seasonal work load, it made a nice balance with the other crops.

In theory, a man could get rich from potatoes. If he grew, say, 10 acres and got 200 bushels to the acre, and he sold them for $1 a bushel, he might gross in a single year half the original cost of his farm. When prices boomed briefly in World War I, some farmers paid for their land with one crop.

But potatoes, like dairy cows, are subject to multiple diseases. They must be sprayed against bugs, which seemed to grow more spray-resistant each year. If the ground is too wet, they scab and are almost worthless. If the season is too dry, they do not grow large enough and both the quality and the quantity of the yield are reduced. Yet, despite the hazards, there was always the possibility of a jackpot, and the farmer, forced to gamble, always tried. In my father's case, the odds seemed always against him. The crop would be too small or the price would be bad. The rich harvest never really came, but it was never further away than the promise of next season.

The harvest is now mechanized, with half a dozen hands doing the work of fifty or a hundred. Machinery has made large-scale operations possible. A farmer may now plant 100 acres of potatoes, cultivate and spray with a single huge tractor, and harvest with the expensive machinery and a minimum of help. One result is that one man makes a living where ten families struggled, and the prices have gone down in the supermarket. But the big fields are lonely places, peopled with the clank of machinery instead of the shouts and groans of youths.

One certain part of the harvest in those days was a potato fight. Perhaps the tongue that hitched the digger to the team would break, and there would be an enforced lull while repairs were made. The devil and energetic boys hate idle hands, and someone would throw one of the little potatoes left behind as a cull, at someone else. No pillow fight could match in hazardous force the fusilade that followed. The weak-hearted would withdraw, the bully would exult, and only the interference of some authority would bring the battle to an end. It was good practice for the snowball season. The girls went in more for vine fights, which were dirtier but left fewer bruises.

In the midst of the back-breaking labor, there was the lure of a social event. You might share a crate with a girl from another farm and pick together, advancing your acquaintance. Or you could talk about girls with the other guys, or talk about your own lives. Potato harvest was part of the social fabric that held the people together, and for lonely farm youths, it was often as much looked forward to for the fun as dreaded for the drudgery. Visits to roller rinks have replaced it, but they are not the same.

In my father's scheme of things, the cows and chickens would provide a living, the hogs occasional pieces of cash, and if the potato crop ever really came through, that would retire the mortgage. It seems little enough to ask for, and it is a shame it never worked out.

Large families were popular, partly because the hands were useful for work but also beause the mortality rate was high. There were eight of us; only one died, seven living to maturity. We were all beset with major ailments that would be dealt with as a matter of routine in the kind of medical care my own children enjoy, but that were mystical threats then.

Perhaps the best example is my own illness. At five, I contracted polio, which we called infantile paralysis. Almost no one understood anything about it. They soaked me in warm water, exercised the muscles, and prayed. For whatever of those reasons, after some sixteen months, I learned to walk again, began school wearing a brace, and eventually shook off most of the effects. Before my children were five, they were innoculated with Salk vaccine as a matter of course and the disease is nearly banished from the nation.

Progress is difficult to define. Had my father's finances been more fortunate, he might say now with some conviction that he lived a fuller life than I. At least the point would be arguable. And it does seem that we lost something when we left the land, something of our roots staying behind, perhaps not to be replaced completely for generations. But in the matter of medical care, I am happy that my children are living now, not then. There is no doubt about that piece of progress.

Most farmers rose earlier than my father. Our neighbor's Jerseys were milked by the time we left the house about seven to round up our cattle. This threw us a bit out of kilter when the time came for projects where work was shared. One family might be ready to go to the field, chores done, by the time the neighbors sat down to breakfast.

Breakfast on the farm is usually overrated by people with selective memories. There were eggs, of course, but no toast; we did not have electricity, and making toast from thick, crusty homemade bread on the back of a wood range is a sometime thing. There was bacon, but it was fatty. The sausage was excellent, but there was rarely quite enough for all the members of a big, hungry family. We ate a lot of oatmeal, forced down us by Mother despite an eternal resistance. If we were lucky, we got brown sugar rather than white. And we always had warm milk, fresh from the cow, still steaming from her body heat. It was unpasteurized, unhomogenized, rich, and yellow, and most of all it was warm.

When I went away to college, the level of food improved for me. I learned that salad dressing did not necessarily mean mayonnaise, and that there was a wealth of foods I had never heard of. But I also learned that most people drank cold milk in the morning, and although I tried to adjust, I never succeeded.

We ate dinner at midday, and it was an improvement over breakfast. There was always lots of it, including all the good bread and fresh butter we wanted. Until World War II, our family churned its own butter, but as prices went up, it actually became cheaper to sell the butterfat to the creamery and buy back the butter. This is because one pound of butterfat, the measure on which our cream checks were based, makes more than one pound of butter.

Supper was at six, and evening chores followed, usually finished by eight. Although that seems like a 13-hour day, there were breaks in it for three meals and it was probably more like a 10-hour hitch.

Somewhere recently I read an article by a learned man who described the normal work year for peasants as running to some 600 hours. Now I think we were in a sense peasants, and 600 hours of work would hardly see us through two summer months. I think the work time for farm adults in my youth would be closer to 50 to 60 hours a week, slightly less in winter and more in summer, with at least 2 or 3 hours every Sunday, a normal work day on

Saturday, not much in the way of vacations. Now and then, my father and mother might get away for a day or two to visit relatives a hundred miles away.

Sociologists make much of the initiation of the young into the various phases of the world of the adult, and properly so. Much of our youth was devoted to a steady initiation process, taking a little more responsibility and a little more work as we grew larger, stronger, more skillful, until the transition to full responsibility seemed so natural it was hardly noticed. In those cases where it came suddenly through accident or tragedy, one was ready for it.

There were plenty of chores, and we grew into them one by one. Early, we learned to "get the cows." Usually we had a dog to help us round up the herd to bring to the barn for the evening milking. My father fetched them in the morning. Responsibility was here; one did not make the cows run, for if their full udders began to sling back and forth they would lose their milk or their tempers. The herd had to be counted, for if a cow was ready to calve, she would slip off by herself and we would have to hunt her down and find the calf. Like many other things about the small dairy herd, bringing them in the evening to the barn was nearly as much ceremony as chore.

One job always resisted was bringing in wood for the two stoves. There was a big wooden box in the back room, and it was to be filled each evening with small wood for the kitchen stove. A boy can do this as soon as he can walk steadily and hold a few sticks in his arms. As you grow bigger and can carry larger loads, the task becomes easier —so much easier that it is referred to as child's play.

FROM THE LAND AND BACK

Big chunks for the heating stove in the living room were to be piled up, and one could not shirk this, because if the chunk pile vanished before bedtime, more would have to be brought in. Again, the work has related to its result—the duty and the reason for the responsibility.

We gathered the eggs when we could be coaxed to and cleaned the chicken coop, another of the hated jobs associated with the hens.

Sometimes, when my son demands his allowance, I wish there was some sort of set chore I could assign him, more meaningful than taking out the garbage or scraping snow from the sidewalk. But the family is not part of the economic unit; I go off to the office to earn my salary, and there is no way for the boys to take part in that. The chore system is essentially make-work, and they cannot feel part of my life in the way I felt part of my father's. I could see him, nearly all day every day, and know what he was doing, and why. We asked "how" a lot, but "why" was always apparent. I never was quite sure how the binder tied a knot around the grain bundles, but I always knew why the bundles were made. My sons know how I go to the office, but it is not so apparent to them why I do it. My explanations must sound made up to them.

As we grew up, we helped milk the cows. This was an important point of progress for the family. If a man can milk six or eight cows, a man with a twelve-year-old son can milk another two or three. And if he has two teen-age sons, he can crowd the herd size up to fifteen or eighteen. The mechanical milker has changed this relationship, not necessarily for the better. We knew rather precisely what kind of contribution we made.

THE LAST GENERATION

The same was true elsewhere on the farm. A man alone had to have help for many things—to put up hay, to fill his silo, to thresh. Even a big family might not furnish labor enough to handle all these tasks without sharing or hiring help, but in some of the bigger families it was close. We could handle our potatoes pretty much ourselves, and, later on, the pickles, a high-labor crop that we grew occasionally in the early 1950s because it had a high cash potential.

You might think the result was exploitation of the child, but nothing could be further from the truth. We took responsibilities eagerly, because it was the clear and obvious way to adulthood, to full partnership. When we could lift a crate full of potatoes, we were moving to stand beside our father, not behind him. We shared in the labor and eventually in the fruits. We grew naturally to adulthood.

Sometimes the father-son relationships I observe on Little League diamonds or at Cub Scout meetings are so pathetically thin by comparison I can scarcely bear to watch. It is as though we are all playing a game, a game which we do not really like much and do not believe in but which we play desperately because we know we should be doing something, and this is the best we can dream up.

When I was perhaps eight or nine, I was strong enough to steer a tractor, if not to work the clutch and brake. On slow summer days, we would hitch the old Farmall F-12 to a stone boat or wagon and go picking stones. The stone boat was simply a flat barge on wooden runners dragged along on a chain. It was used for stone picking because the bed was only 6 inches or so off the ground, and large rocks could be easily rolled on to it. My father would start the tractor, set it in a low gear at slow throttle, and set a general course. I could stand behind the big iron steering wheel, guiding the tractor toward the rocks, turning as directed, while my father and older brothers rolled the stones on until the boat was filled and could be taken to the nearest stone pile for dumping.

When my son was eight, he enrolled in Cub Scouts, and on the night he won his first medal, I stood beside him in the elementary school gymnasium, pinned the Wolf Badge on his uniform, and shook his hand. He had done some simple things; tied a knot, whittled a toy, memorized some lines from the Wolf Book. What did it all mean? Nothing, really, except he was proud that he had done it and I am proud of him when he does anything he is proud of. I am very sorry that he cannot drive the tractor while I pick stones, and so is he. The Wolf Badge is not progress.

It was this sense of involvement in a common mission that made the life so whole for children. There was no alienation, for we all worked together to make the farm complete.

But while this involvement drew the family together in a way that many families now achieve only by camping in the summer or in some other made-up manner, it also produced a narrow vision of life, and the shock felt by young people when they went out into the world was profound. The narrowness arose because this world of the farm was self-contained, insulated and insulating, so full, so demanding of attention and effort, that it was hard to see how anything else mattered. Through the years of the 1930s, when the world lurched along toward war, we had no knowledge of it. Until Pearl Harbor compelled our attention, the farm world was the whole world, to be defended against New York or Washington as much as against Berlin.

The narrowness had a healthy, enduring effect, however. It was the reverse of the kind of influence wrought by the intense education of a physician, say, or an engineer. The rigorous demands those educations put on men seem to have a confining effect, with graduates in such disciplines rarely able to break free to the broader interests more common in those who have a liberal education. They are confined by their training; the boy on the farm was broadened by his, for he was almost forced to learn how things are, and how they work. Being raised on a general farm before the days of technology and automation was like being raised in a laboratory, with opportunity for the nourishment of every curiosity.

We learned geometry from seeing how a corner fence-post is braced to make it rigid. By the time I was ten, I suppose, I had fixed in my mind the way to tie those posts together with wire, twist the wire with a stick, and make a strong structure, as tidy and as intregal as a suspension bridge, though vastly simpler. Why it worked was obvious to us, because we built it and could see what happened. We built a shed, and I saw how the rafters were braced to make a frame that could not give unless the timbers were shattered lengthwise, an impossibility. Later, when I struggled with plane geometry in a remedial course in college, I tried to explain this to the instructor. Triangular angles worked because there was nothing else for them to do. He wanted theorems, however, so I memorized enough to pass his course, but I didn't believe them. I believed in strong corner posts.

We saw how water came down the hill from the windmill to the stock tank, bubbling out as the wind turned the pump, and how it rose higher if the pipes were small and less high if the pipes were higher. We knew why the windmill worked one way and not another, and toy plastic windmills had little interest for us, because we had the real thing.

The machinery was simple enough that we could understand it, and there was time. No boy with any curiosity at all can sit on a haymower for hours at an end, with nothing to do but raise the sickle bar at the corners, without understanding perfectly how every motion of the machine is converted into the back-and-forth cutting action. If you watch a plow turn the soil, you see how the sod holds it together and which weeds or grasses are strong and which weak and how they tuck under the plow. You learn how a side-delivery hay rake gently slides the alfalfa to the side for gathering, or how a disk or harrow works, or a cultivator, or the angles for turning a wagon or a trailer or, later on, a truck.

Boys who have played baseball or basketball through all their childhood have a store of knowledge they do not even know they possess. Farm boys do too, and it is a priceless warehouse of information about the way things work.

The information is about animals, too, about how they get along and what their place is; and about the seasons, and what they do for the land and the things that grow on it; and about nature, too, and the way she likes things to be.

Most youths have at some time the feeling of being out after a rain, sensing that the air is clean and the grass is reaching out for a new look at the sky. A walk through the corn or hay or wheat is a multiple of that feeling. The most avid sports fan is the man with money on the game; the farmer's money is on the weather and on nature, and the odds are at best only slightly in his favor.

In that part of Michigan hail shreds the corn crop every ten or fifteen years. It is a sudden thing, usually following a long drouth. The sky will fill with clouds, and the air will take on that curious light brilliance that it has when the ozone is in a slightly higher balance and the atmosphere is pregnant with a storm. Then the hail comes, and it usually lasts only ten or fifteen minutes. What was a field of corn, thick green leaves and sturdy stalks, reaching up with the tassels not yet showing and the ears not formed, is suddenly an empty place, with no leaves, few stalks, and no promise any more.

The wheat is usually a little further along at hailstorm time. The hail will thresh it out, the not quite ripe kernels will cover the ground, and there is nothing to do but to mow it down and try again another year.

Many men love the land. Some love the challenge of competing with nature for a living. These are the men who weep after a hailstorm, because they have been put in their place, humbled and humiliated as the thoughtless slap humbles the child who dares too much.

Nature is absolutely indiscriminate about her little temper tantrums. She will send a belt of hail a couple hundred yards wide across a county sometimes, and it might cut across one farm and only dampen a hay field while it destroys a neighbor's crop. Often, after such a storm, the farmers will drift into town, eager to hear each other tell whether he was spared or ruined, gossiping like old women at the well hearing about the battle of a distant legion.

So we lived with nature, and we came to understand her generosity or caprice, and we grew up with a silent knowledge such as that the sailor has of the sea, or the pilot of the sky.

But what did we know of anything else? We did not know of cities, for instance, and the stories of the "hick" coming to the city to be taken by his slicker cousins are all true. It is more difficult to lie to your neighbor on the farm, for he is likely to be your neighbor for half a century, and perhaps your most regular contact with another human being. If you have lied, he will find out sooner or later. And if you cheat him, he will remember. We were not well prepared to live an urban life, where human relationships are so often secondary relationships at best, and so rarely lasting.

Nor had we any preparation for the wide knowledge of the university. As a junior, I encountered a political science professor who nearly worked me to death. He was possessed of great knowledge in a multitude of areas that I had not even known existed. I was ashamed and determined to know all about them. He would give a lecture on the politics of Burma, and I would furiously read up on Burma so that next time I would be ready for him. And he would go on to India, and I would have to catch up all over again. It was more than the experience of an awakening intellectual curiosity; it was the experience of finding new worlds that I had never heard of.

And what did we know of social life in the city? We had had our friends forever, and no one had warned us that we might have to go out from that place and make new friends in a new place where we made a living. We were shy by experience, slow to meet people, easy to exploit. The farm had been a physics laboratory but the city needs the social laboratory of the streets.

There are long stretches of solitude on a farm, and I think the big families are partly an unconscious effort to make it impossible to ever be lonely again. But there are long times to talk, if you are fortunate enough to have an articulate father. Mine was, in matters of the farm, if not a man given to much thought on broader affairs. So we talked incessantly about our plans for the future; what we would plant in this field, the possible crop-rotation patterns, the livestock and the barn and the buildings and the tractor and the machinery and the woods and the weather. If we are sometimes bored with each other now, it is because we said so much so long ago.

The solitude bred diffidence in personal relations. We were shy about touching one another, shy in asking about personal matters. It is easy to talk to a stranger, because you do not expect to meet again. It is more difficult to risk offending a man who may be your major companion in all your work time for several decades.

Yet we broke through that somewhat, relishing the

rough play with our father as much as any child. We grew shy with one another later on.

Somehow, despite the grinding poverty of the 1930s, I think those were happy years for my parents. The children came, and though we all ran up medical bills that could never be paid, we were together and gave a hope for the future. My father talked much about how he looked forward to having us around him, how he hoped that the barn would someday carry the name "Stadtfeld and Sons," and then—and I think he looked forward to this more than to the first—"Stadtfeld Brothers."

In fact, the barn was never painted at all. The good potato crop never came. It always rained too little to make good beans, or too much to harvest them. We never had so many heifer calves that the herd grew large and made us wealthy. We were always just getting by.

Yet there was always hope, always a genuine belief that things would be better. After all, we were all sharing the same work, dreaming the same dream.

And then came the war, and so many things were pulled apart that were never put back together again. The fabric of that life tore, and we looked back from the other side of the rent and wondered how it ever worked in the first place, how it ever held together. It would be years before I understood.

3. ONE NEIGHBOR

He must have been young once and played with clay marbles and kites. But I cannot imagine him so, for his steadiness of spirit and his sure feel for his place in the world were such that he seemed to have been always old and gentle and wise, with a weathered dignity that set him apart a little from those around him.

His many sons and daughters called him "Pa," the only family in the area to use that name rather than "Pop" or "Dad." Our parents somehow never had to stress to us that we were always to call him Mr. Wagner, never by his first name. It did not occur to any of us to be familiar with him.

FROM THE LAND AND BACK

Adults who called him by his first name said "Otto" with an air of holding hats in hand while they talked to him. He had something of learning and knowledge about him, he wore a cap, not a hat, and he held a simple and complete vision of the nature of things.

With his will, he set the limits of the world he would live in and within those dimensions he was as free as a man can be, for he took orders only from his God and he interpreted those orders himself. There was nothing of the hustler in him. He lived always in the tiny world bounded by the line fences of his own 80 acres, extending regularly to the church a quarter-mile away and rarely to the town or county seat. He was poor, and natural, and very wise and complete.

He was a magnetic neighbor, drawing us across the road to him because he was somehow fascinating. He did not play with children, his own or others. If we joined him, it was always on his terms, and he often made it plain that he did not want us along. He once spanked me and sent me home when he found that I had not told my mother where I was. He owned a copy of *Ben Hur*, and once in the winter, when he sat with his feet on the open oven door in his kitchen, red-toed high woolen socks warming, I asked him to tell me the story. He told me bluntly that it was too old for me.

Close neighbors were not in great supply, and if we were to break out of the confines of our own family for company we had to cultivate whoever was there. We would probably have spent a lot of time with him under any circumstances short of clear hostility, but in fact this strong old soul was quite a different personality from my own father, who was usually exuberant with hopes and plans, and it was an attractive change to hang around with him.

His peace of soul and contentment with a limited life were not passed on to his children. All but two of them hurried to escape as far away as possible. Then ran to cities and factories, to the bright lights and the automobiles, to a faster pace. They fled the things all farm boys flee—the dull monotony, the simple life that seems so attractive to many of us now in comparison with the plastic society, the cold harsh concrete and Neon, the endless, meaningless assembly line. Old Otto had drawn on generations of peasant wisdom to build his satisfaction. His children, and his neighbor's children, have not yet had time to develop the urban equivalent.

He was a dictator in his little life-support system, the ruling patriarch. Because it was so self-contained, its members were so dependent on it that their father had the casual authority of a ship's captain. As the children grew to adulthood, they were ready to jump ship in any strange port just for the chance to escape, the possibility of adventure, the challenge of being on their own.

The life that fulfilled him, and bored his children, centered on what was really close to a subsistence farm, largely outside the money economy. He had little money and needed little. The theme was self-reliance, self-subsistence, as complete as possible, in soul and body.

His farm was 80 acres, and it was on the average miserable land. It fronted a quarter of a mile wide on a state

highway—now paved, then thinly graveled—and ran
south for half a mile, with woods across the back and just a
corner of a little lake intruding on the southwest line. A
stream angled through the front part, purling along west to
east. Between the stream and the road, and for a short way
south of the stream, there was something that might once
have been a flood land was reasonably fertile. Then the
farm broke sharply upward, with the rear half of the
cleared land bucking up and down in formidable clay
knobs of questionable fertility, only marginally approacha-
ble with horse-drawn implements. So he had perhaps 30
acres of reasonably manageable, fairly fertile land; 35 acres
of clay knobs, and some woods and a little bit of lake. The
way he farmed it, it was enough.

A word about the soil. The red clay that pokes up on
these knobs is really subsoil. It is on the surface because the
glacier was gasping and stuttering when it retreated across
that part of Michigan. It was scraping away the good soil
one day, dropping rocks in heaps the next, leaving a landscape that was forever to bounce up and down like an
ocean in storm. Of course the tops of the hills eroded over
the years. What good soil there was wound up in the valleys and down the streams in the next county. What was
left on those points was a red earth that is hostile to man
and tillage. Nature meant it to stay put, and it was hard
work to move it around.

This red clay is a highly expansible soil, which means it
swells mightily when wet. The granules of sandy soil allow
water to run through them without being much affected.
The rich soil of the corn belt, or in southern Michigan or

in Michigan's "thumb" region, has high proportions of organic matter, the result of grass building for eons a rich mulch, making the soil black and rich. The organic matter soaks up water, and holds it, and the result is a nearly ideal seedbed, as you can see by the lush crops when you look along any road in those areas in late summer.

Clay is, to put it mildly, less hospitable to the farmer. It soaks up water well, but when wet it is heavy, sticky, unworkable. When dry, it becomes exactly like rock. This is not hyperbole. I recall looking at the surface of soils at the bottom of small water puddles. As the water evaporates, the surface cracks in the sun. Dark lowland soil with lots of organic matter is soft and almost fluffy. Clay soil, on the other hand, is so hard when it dries that the little squares left between cracks can be used for ashtrays. When we had no money to buy marbles, we made them from this clay, and if they were made carefully, they would stand up to nearly as much snapping and cracking as the store-bought kind.

So clay is usually either too wet or too dry. The farmer's only hope is to hit it in those few days in the spring when the moisture is just right. In the days when he worked with horses and a team might plow an acre a day, it was virtually impossible to complete the tillage of more than three or four acres before the ideal moisture level passed. On the rest of the field, a horse-drawn plow would rut and scrape along, and there would be only a few inches of badly tilled soil for the seedbed. The result was not favorable to high yields of crops.

Later, when we got tractors, the timing was slightly better. But I have seen tractors straining away as if in agony, dragging along heavy tillage equipment that could shatter pavement, as the farmer tried desperately to break up the clay and plant his crops in it. At its best, this is expensive. At its worst, it was heartbreaking. Imagine this clay, piled in steep short hills, and a man trying to till it with a team of horses that must rest often from the hard work, and you have a notion of the challenge faced by the desperate men who tried to wrench a crop from it.

If the tillage is good and the planting timely, the rewards can be impressive. The clay can push up wheat yielding 60 bushels to the acre and oats yielding 80; once alfalfa is rooted, it will grow as hardy and high as sweet clover, waist high by mid-June, so dense you can hardly walk through it. Sometimes, it would be so lush it would topple of its own weight. The big alfalfa roots burrow so deep and grow so thick that when after a few years the sod was turned for corn the roots would cause the plow point to skid aside as though it had hit a rock. If the seed is planted at the right time, the clay wraps itself around it as a woman wraps herself around her lover, keeping the seed nourished and safe from the elements. But the clay is always a reluctant mistress, and no one ever got rich on a clay-hill farm.

The southwest corner of Otto's farm sloped down into a lake—an odd, even sinister little lake of perhaps 5 or 10 acres. The north edge was swampy and dribbled off into a marl bed. Marl is a deposit of clay mixed with calcium carbonate. This was not bad marl, as marl goes—now and then, somebody or other had made attempts to dig it for spreading on the field to make the soil sweet. The use of marl for this had preceded the use of lime. The object is to reduce the acidity of the soil, to make it more congenial to hay and grain crops. Sour soil does not produce crops well; it may even be taken over by nasty little weeds which thrive in that sort of soil, one of the plants nature has evolved to keep the earth covered against the elements. By now it has certainly been more than thirty years since anyone tried to dig marl out of that pit. This was a soggy, sloppy business; one scooped the marl into manure spreaders and spread it around the fields. In the 1930s, the federal government made limestone available cheaply, and the marl business died without anyone's feeling very bad about it. It may not have helped the soil much anyway.

On Otto's end of the lake, a crude dock of poles and planks poked out into the water. The edges of the lake were mucky and weedy, and at the dock the water was some 10 feet deep. A clumsy old boat, with square ends, similar to those called johnboats and used for simple fishing on rivers in Missouri, was tied there. Otto would often go back to the lake on summer afternoons, or in the early evening after chores were done, and with a bamboo pole, a line, and a few worms, catch a mess of fish—bass, bluegills, some pike. These were kept alive in a bucket; he would trudge back to the house and put the bucket in the stock tank where the fish would live until they were cleaned for the table.

As children, we used to creep into the dark old well house and peer into the tank to see what fish were there. Now and then, there would be a big pike, which we thought looked like a shark, or even a sunfish, flashing in the dark water. The stock didn't mind sharing the water and the fish seemed to keep the tank clean. He kept minnows in the tank, too—for bait.

Much more interesting to us were the lake's turtles and their lore. The turtles were real. Sometimes we could catch them with fish spears, impaling them through the neck, hauling them into the boat, gingerly nudging them into a potato crate, and lugging them to the house. Mrs. Wagner would clean them and brew turtle soup. Local lore had it that different parts of the turtles tasted like the meat of different farm animals. My father's response to this was sarcastic. "Yes," he would say, "you can have ram, ham, lamb, sheep, or mutton."

The lore had to do with huge turtles and fish said to live deep in the cold dark waters of the lake. We were all certain that on occasion we had glimpsed fish as long as the rowboat or turtles so big they could have dragged the boat under. No such monsters were ever caught, but we used to talk about putting dynamite in the lake to stun these creatures so they would float to the surface.

One of the few fishing excursions I ever enjoyed was going out with a light and a spear after dark in the early spring, just after the ice was off the lake. It was exciting, and to be out on the lake in the dark with friends was pleasant. It was also illegal, I think, but we never paid much attention to fishing seasons or rules on what we considered our private lake.

In the winter, the lake provided ice for the next summer. We cut it in big blocks, carefully stored them in the ice house, packed with sawdust, and took them down for ice cream or cold drinks the next year, knowing very definitely how precious the ice was.

But if we did not know how real the monsters in the lake were, we knew full well about the snakes. The thing I remember best about that farm was the snakes. Sometimes they seemed to be all over. They ranged from bright little garter snakes around the barn and in the fields to thick ugly black snakes in the stream and huge striped or spotted snakes around the lake.

As a boy, I developed a galloping case of herpetophobia. I have never been able to isolate any event which caused this, but it made much of my time on this farm a fairly intense hell. It was not unusual to find a snake curled on the dock, taking the sun, preventing me from making my way to the boat. Even if I threw a stick and frightened the snake away, it would take me minutes to find the courage to run along the dock and jump the place where it had been in order to reach the boat. Sometimes, when we went back to swim, a lovely snake would be there before us. Someone else would have to scare it away. I swear I once saw a brilliant snake at least 6 feet long stretched on the rock along the stream by the bridge as I drove by on the tractor. I swear I saw it, and I can remember it today, but I am not sure I really saw it.

There was little patience for such foolishness. When Otto's son had taken over the farm after World War II, I often helped him. We were determined to end my silly fear, and one day we set out to bring in grain from shocks in the back field that sloped down to the lake. I took the job of standing on the ground, pitching the bundles of wheat (or oats) from the shock to the wagon. All day long, each time I stuck the fork into a bundle and raised it up, a snake would fall out to slither away. I was determined to see the ordeal through and did so, but the next time I saw a snake, I jerked a little. It had done no good, and it had filled my nights with hideous dreams.

Summer was sometimes a long nightmare, with snakes crawling up the windrow of hay, over the loader, and falling onto the wagon where I was working. Or coming out of the mow, hurrying across the barn floor at top speed, trying to escape us. I was glad to let them go; they had nothing to fear from me. Sometimes, my instinct to destroy the innocent things would take over, and I would beat one to death with a hay fork. This usually resulted in breaking the fork handle, at least costing money for a new handle, and at worst delaying the work. I suffered from nightmares about them, and recently, when my son found a little snake and brought it home, I found it impossible to explain my fear. I know now and I knew then that they are harmless. We lived too far north in Michigan to encounter the state's only poisonous snake, the Massasauga rattler. But this was not and is not a rational fear. I could face an angry Holstein bull weighing 3,000 pounds, but a snake would send me up a ladder. They occupy a little sworl in a dark corner of my brain, always ready to give a quick shock to my nervous system.

Otto's farm was the most self-contained unit I ever knew. He had stock for every use, and a separate building for most purposes—seven, not counting the privy.

Closest to the house was the woodshed, where fuel for the winter's heating and the year's cooking was stored. It was a wooden frame building. Fishing gear was kept in the loft, and in the summer fish were cleaned either there or on the big concrete back porch. The floor was probably dirt, but years of splitting and chopping wood had built up such a litter that the surface was inches deep in shavings and chips.

Three kinds of wood came from this shed. The first was in big chunks—the size of a small tree trunk, or a big one split only once or twice. These were carried to the basement to stoke the furnace. We envied the Wagners this central heating plant; we made do at home with a big heating stove in the living room. Besides providing more heat, the furnace would hold a fire all night. A damper control extended up through the floor to the living room with a chain device similar to those used on a ship's pilot house for signaling the boiler room. We played with it for that purpose—in the summer only, for woe be to anyone who tampered with it in the winter and upset the flow of heat.

In addition to the heater chunks, there was the smaller wood for the kitchen range—small limbs or finely split wood. Though it seemed simple enough at the time, I marvel now at the way farm women could heat these crude stoves so that they would cook and bake, heat water, and heat the kitchens. Naturally most of these activities continued without pause through the summer, with the result that the kitchens were incredibly hot, especially in the canning season.

The third kind of wood was kindling—fine sticks, boy-scout dry, for starting fires if they went out.

Also next to the dwelling was the well house, topped by

a lumbering windmill. The stock was watered from there, simply enough in summer, by drinking from a tank, but a wretched winter job, involving breaking the ice off the water or building a fire in a little wood stove to thaw it. In central–northern Michigan, you always find stock tanks in little houses. Later on we put water into the barns. For most of us, that happened in the mid-to-late 1940s.

Back of the woodshed was a grape arbor, now long gone. It was a shady, strange place to play, especially at dusk. I honestly do not know whether Otto made wine from the grapes or just ate them. He did make cider, but I doubt that he deliberately fermented it for an intoxicant.

There were two more buildings to the south and west of the well house. The first was a tool shed, dirt-floored, air-leaking; its only purpose being to put a roof over the expensive equipment—the grain binder, the mower, and the tillage implements—that would rust if left out. Along the north wall were the car license plates from years back. It smelled of oil and gasoline and, in the summer, of cheap prison-made binder twine.

South, toward the barn, was the chicken coop. Perhaps 15 by 30 feet, it was made of stone picked up from the farm. Low ceilings helped the chickens keep it warm in winter. Long poles, cut from saplings, formed roosts. The ammonia smell in summer made your eyes water.

Otto would sometimes take an egg, break a tiny hole in one end, and suck it dry as he walked around the buildings on chore rounds. I once asked if I could have one. My first taste convinced me that I had made a mistake. I wanted to throw it away. But that would have been waste. He stood

over me until I finished the egg. It was thirty years before
I could face another egg yolk.

The southwest building in the quadrangle was the hog
house—another stone building, but with a peaked roof.
It had a loft, stuffed with straw for insulation. I suppose if
we had been different families, or if ages had been closer,
first sex experiences might have taken place there. The
small wouldn't have bothered us. I am not sure why nothing of the sort happened.

The back door of the hog house swung out to a little lot
that ran down to the creek. Swing is the right word.
Hog house doors hinge so that the hogs can run through
and the door will fall shut behind them. As small children
were being taught to close house doors, mothers would call
out, "Were you raised in a hog house, where the doors
swing shut by themselves?" This was, by the way, a
snake-free place. Hogs attack and kill snakes. I do not
know why, though I always thought snakes to be high in
protein, and hogs are very smart about balancing their
diets.

The main barn was big for such a small farm. Many
barns were built into a bank, so that the entry to the
threshing floor was on the second level. The barnyard here
was too flat for that, so the barn had to be larger. The
thresh floor was entered from the west, with mows on
both sides. The east half of the barn was two-story. The
lower half housed the cattle, and the upper half was blown
full of straw from the thresher so the straw could be
pushed down through the holes directly into box stalls.
Hay had to be dragged in from the west side.

FROM THE LAND AND BACK

We handled that hay a lot of times. It was mowed by a machine, then bunched with a dump rake. Handwork was required to make those bunches into round piles, the size of a big fork load. The piles were tossed onto a wagon, the load divided into layers by rope and slat slings. The load was then hauled to the barn, where the horses were un-hitched, led out singly beside the wagon, and hitched again to a big rope. This rope was connected through pulleys to the track at the top of the barn and down to hooks that raised the sling loads of hay so they could be shunted into the mows and dumped. Handwork was required to move the hay around in the mows, so they filled more or less evenly. In the winter, the hay had to be dragged from the mows and dumped into the threshing floor, then dragged again into the stable.

My father used a side-delivery rake, which put the hay in windrows. A loader then moved it up to the wagon for loading, and the rest of the system was the same. In the 1940s, Otto's son acquired a side-delivery rake and loader. It was another ten years before we all took to baling the hay.

We put up 20 to 30 tons of hay on each farm this way each summer. It was one of the reasons we did not require artificial muscle-building courses.

Otto's Jerseys stood close together, side by side, in a dozen handmade wooden stanchions. Each cow stuck her head between two upright planks, one fixed, the other hinged at the bottom on a bolt so that it could be swung closed to keep the cow in her place. They were held shut by wooden chocks that dropped down from the top. More prosperous farms had steel stanchions, which were hung top and bottom on chains to give the cow a little more freedom. But the wood was somehow warmer, and worn smooth over the years, generations of Jerseys rubbing it to a smooth polish. A wooden manger in front held hay, silage, or grain. The cows stood on concrete, padded with straw. The bedding was changed daily, and the gutter was scooped out with fork and shovel each morning.

The wooden silo served through the 1930s and was replaced in the late 1940s with a new concrete-stave unit, larger to handle food for more cows. The land was pressed harder to feed more cows, and today the milk herd approaches twenty on occasion, producing milk checks as high as a thousand dollars a month from feed wrenched from those reluctant acres.

Across the aisle from the manger were the box stalls, for dry cows, heifers growing up to replace cows, and sometimes, in the years before artificial breeding, a bull.

As Otto and his sons walked up to the house after milking, carrying the fresh rich milk for separating, they passed the smoke house, full of the inviting odors of curing ham and sausage in season.

Architecturally and socially, the family's house was not as important as the barn. It was built mostly of stone from the farm and it had a big dining room where the family could gather around the huge table, but for the most part it was a cramped little affair, with low ceilings and bedrooms that were small but numerous enough for the many children. The attic space was usually appropriated by the eldest for a bedroom, although it was unheated in winter and a furnace in summer, because it was the most interesting place in the house, and the most private.

The cellar was neat and well kept. There were bins for apples, potatoes, and various fruits, for coal, and for the different sizes of woods for the different stoves . . . bins like pigeon holes, a place for everything, the entire cellar small and swept and tidy, appropriate for the life style of the master of the house.

At the back of the farm, where the hills sloped down to the lake, a root cellar was dug into the hill at a steep place. Rutabagas, potatoes, sometimes the big winter radishes were kept there, the land protecting them from the cold with its bulk. The cellar fell into disuse over the years and is probably abandoned now, save for an occasional woodchuck or mouse trying to establish squatter's rights.

It is important, perhaps more important than anything else about that farm and its owner, that there was a stile in the corner of the barnyard, beside the big pole gate to the lane leading back to the fields and the lake.

It was not a fancy stile, only three boards high, in easy steps over the fence. Down on the field side, it let onto a path that connected, in a few feet, to the path the cows had worn through the years, off to the side from the main tracks where the wagons and implements and later the tractor ran.

Cow paths are a matter of some interest. Students wear paths across the campuses of colleges and universities, beating down the grass, defying all barriers, ignoring all sidewalks. Student paths have two things in common: they are invariably the shortest distance between two points, and they are straight. Cow paths are neither. They always wander and turn a little, and never go straight to the object. It is as though some sense of balance keeps cows not on a path of direction, but on a route that maintains the elevation and thus the pressure on their ears. Yet cow paths wind up and down hills, too. So perhaps the reason is that the animals like to turn a little as they walk, enjoying a slightly different angle to the scenery, a little variation of sights. Humans take the straight route, intent not on the journey but on the destination. We largely miss the trip, thinking ahead to a future time. Cows do not think ahead, and perhaps they see more of the countryside. Their paths are unhurried, and more fun. Once they are cut into the sod, they are never changed.

But why a stile to reach this path? A moment's effort would swing open the gate. Children and reasonably agile adults could duck through the bars. In the strictest physical terms, to climb and descend the stile may have taken more effort than to open the gate. And one rarely, if ever, passed that barrier with hands burdened to complicate the passage. It was a route one took on the way to the lake to fish or swim, on the way to get the cows—and the gate would have to be opened for them—or simply to join someone in the fields.

Yet Otto had measured the fence, sawed the steps, built the framework, and provided the stile. Hours of work went into the project—perhaps it took a day. To save an occasional second of time? To save wear and tear on the pole gate?

He has been dead now for more than twenty years, and

FROM THE LAND AND BACK

I cannot ask him. The stile was long since torn away when the gate was widened to make room for the passing of bigger machinery. So I can only guess. And I believe he built that stile because it seemed proper to build it, because it somehow completed the tidiness of the farmyard enclosure, perhaps because as a boy somewhere he had crossed a stile in a farm lane and he built his own to fill out the picture he held in his mind of the way a barnyard fence should be, with a stile to pass beside the gate. He may have once kissed a girl on a stile or perhaps only held her hand to help her across. He was a private man, and never told, if he was ever asked. But I think he had some dim reason not covered with rational explanations, just as we edge the lawns along our sidewalks, for example, or trim our shrubs to make even hedges, in some unquestioned way making complete and right the picture we carry in our heads of the way things should be.

It may have been because that picture was so singularly his, so little shared or discussed with his family, that the social and economic system he built did not survive him. For his solitude alone made him in a sense a tyrannical figure. His habit of narrowing his vision to an area no broader than the space around him made him forget to include others in the planning, and his boys grew up believing that he dozed when in fact he must have dreamed. His was a little world that did not survive the day of the big operator.

When I was a child, I used to watch him cobble shoes and I badgered him to teach me. It was the sort of fascinating thing he knew so well—little things, crucial for the good life in a simple society. He knew how to repair old shoes, shear sheep, caulk a boat, lay a stone wall, make sausage, which fish to put in the stock tank to keep it clean. But what he taught me, and that posthumously, was to talk to my children. For if he had shared better with his, they might have understood themselves sooner.

As was common in those days, the world changed too quickly for him. The depression was no major event. A farm essentially outside the money economy is less affected by Wall Street than is a corporation. Those long years between the wars were a time of milking the Jerseys, slopping the hogs, fighting the clay for corn enough to feed the cows and pigs, raising the children, fishing in the evenings, and walking up the hill to church on Sunday.

He bought a Model A Ford but never learned to drive it. Indeed, he would rather not ride in it if it could be avoided. He bought a trailer for it to use for hauling stock to market. One of his boys drove. A neighbor half a mile away had a Jersey bull, and the old man would lead the cows over the hill for breeding. The road is a two-lane rural raceway now; a farmer takes his life in his hands when he ventures on it with a high-speed tractor. It would be suicidal for either man or beast to stroll alongside it.

He farmed without a tractor, largely because he did not really trust them. His hills were steep and tractors tipped over. He would hire a neighbor for some plowing, trying to get that beastly clay turned over so he could plant it. He did not buy a milking machine. His dependence on big machinery was confined to the grain thresher and the silo filler, both of which were owned and operated on a communal basis.

FROM THE LAND AND BACK

Basically, he was not attracted by machinery, equipment, and technology in general. He had a peasant's combination of distrust and lack of interest in them. It was one of the key breaking points between his way of life and what followed. A farmer is as fascinated with machinery as a factory worker with his car, though both often turn out to be self-serving bitch goddesses. That particular passion was not one that gnawed old Otto.

World War II came, and he was passively patriotic if never political. Years later, studying Asian communism, I came across a saying attributed to the Chinese. As I recall it, it ran: "When the sun comes up in the morning, the farmer goes out to the field. When the sun goes down, the farmer comes home. What has the king to do with that?" But after Pearl Harbor, Roosevelt had much to do with Otto's life. His sons went off to war. We prayed for peace and victory. Otto's wife hung her flag in the window with three blue stars. A neighbor's son was captured when the Germans surged back through the Ardennes forest, but he was freed and came home.

Otto's boys came home to the 20-20 rehabilitation programs; they had $20 a week for twenty weeks while they tried to forget Iwo Jima and Tarawa. I was a child, and I had a child's glorious view of the war, gleaned from comic books and imagination. I wanted the boys to tell me all about how wonderful it was, and they wanted to drink beer and tinker with the old cars they acquired and sleep late and, please God, to forget. They had brought the world home with them.

ONE NEIGHBOR

They used to hang around our house, enjoying my father's sympathy and tolerance, both abounding by comparison with their father who wanted them to settle down as quickly as possible. One evening, I slipped a prankster's little explosive charge into a cigarette and lighted it for one of Otto's boys, who had lived through the hell of the island campaigns. The tiny explosion made him turn green and yellow and terribly silent, and I was so horrified at what I had done that I never nagged at him for war stories again.

One of Otto's sons took over the farm, accepting it as a gift in return for caring for Otto and his wife as long as they lived. It was not an uncommon arrangement but was known as a expensive way to buy a farm.

The son and his bride remodeled the house, putting in a bathroom and a water heater. Otto used to spit tobacco in the bathroom sink. His daughter-in-law thought at such times that he was a filthy old man, but he simply thought it was still his house, still his place.

Otto had tried to live with the clay; we tried to subdue it. He had learned to accept his world; we tried to conquer it. He fished more, though he could no longer haul the boat out of the water in the fall and caulk it himself. He kept quiet about the changes that went on around the farm. There were more cows, more machinery, more noise, a new crop of children. He kept his own counsel, as he had always done, and it was difficult to know when he approved and when he did not. A generation or so earlier, he would have been the ruling elder, his counsel sought and his word respected. But machinery broke his continu-

(77)

ity with the way the land was farmed, and short courses from the state agricultural college undermined his knowledge.

Before long, the old ways were all gone. Where he had looked in, we looked out. Our dreams were placed in the future; our pictures of the way things ought to be were built on photographs in the *Michigan Farmer* and *Hoard's Dairyman*, not on a dim simple image of peasant Europe. We became modern. We became American, introduced to the world. And like all who come late to join an already complex society, we were its victims before we could be its beneficiaries.

He lived on in the new life, gray and quiet, sucking the milk off his cereal noisily through his mustache. Suddenly I stopped asking him anything except the whereabouts of his son. I have no memory of his death.

4. THE FABRIC
OF FRIENDSHIP

In the old life we were bound together by a feeling of community, not torn apart as we may be today by feelings of division. There was no arrogance of power, for there was no power, save in nature. There was no impudence of wealth or station, for we were all new to the country, and poor. My grandfather had his name on a stained glass window he had donated to the church, and there may have been no higher sign of stature than that. Yet my father never even mentioned it to me, and when I noticed it one day and inquired if that was my grandfather, he said it was, but I could tell by his tone that it had no special importance.

This levelness of station, along with the closeness of farm life itself, made people gentle toward one another. This was partly because we had the opposite of territorial pressure—we had just a little too much space, were always a bit intimidated by nature, a little lonely most of the time, grateful for companionship when it was available, cautious of giving offense.

Always there was room to be alone, truly alone, to escape in space or in place of work from neighbors or family or friends, so the noise a neighbor might make would be welcome as a friendly sound because it was reassuring rather than intrusive. Much of the time, our work forced us to be apart, to be alone for hours on end with our thoughts, so we were happy to see our family again at 6 o'clock, and delighted to see a neighbor.

Another reason was the special respect people have for one another when their families have been acquainted for generations, when they are likely to be related, when they expect to share line fences and church pews for some generations to come. It is fascinating to see the incredible impersonal rudeness that descends on man in a traffic jam, perhaps as he is trying to get out of a parking lot after a football game or a play. He is safe in his steel capsule, and though another human being with whom he shared a pleasurable experience just a few minutes before is only inches away, the isolation of the automobile enables him to shed his humanity and be sublimely selfish. Such an attitude was not possible on the farm, because of people's respect for one another, and for the condition of space and loneliness they shared.

Take the matter of line fences. In the days when a farmer might want to pasture any field, it was important that his neighbor do his share in keeping up the line fence. The rule was that a man was responsible for the half of the fence on his right as he stood facing the neighbor's property. Keeping up the fences could be a source of conflict, but we found that they joined as much as they separated. If cows breached either half, it was a time to help set things straight, to get together, help patch up the damage, to talk a little. The poet Robert Frost's farmer was right; good fences do make good neighbors. But good neighbors make good fences, too, and they talk across them, and they share a mutual respect over them.

This social closeness, this respect for the other's place, influenced our attitude toward people, and it helped create our humor. It was a natural humor, often earthy, sometimes vulgar. Some of it was highly subtle, the product of good minds with plenty of time to work on the turning of a phrase. But it was never vicious. It turned our problems around, and, like the songs of the black man in the South, it helped us bear our burdens.

To be honest about it, it helped us bear one another, too. For in balance with the respect for one another's feelings there was a tacit acknowledgment that as far as neighbors and companions were concerned, we had to make do with what was at hand.

FROM THE LAND AND BACK

It helped us bear a neighbor, whom I shall call Amos, who was odd enough to be called an eccentric. Actually, he had only a half-serving of the eccentricity that comes from living back in the woods alone for a long, long time. He had a family that kept him from flipping all the way out. He had, in fact, a pretty daughter who could have kept me on the farm had she showed a bit more interest at the proper time, and he had a very straight wife and they kept him steady.

One late fall evening we were at the cider mill he ran as a side line. He and my father were talking in the yard, sharing that reluctance to part that is common to men whose circle of friends is too small. As they talked a car drove by, kicking up a cloud of dust on the road which was really a sand trail, uncluttered with gravel. Amos ran to the road to watch the car go by, then returned to continue the conversation. A second car passed only a few minutes later, and as he ran back from watching he exclaimed in some excitement to my father, "My God, Taft, my God, civilization is creeping up on us."

But it was Amos's closest neighbor who was the true eccentric, and who was without doubt an authentic genius. His children were all bright to the point of being strange; those who have channeled their intelligence have made names for themselves in various fields. One shared a chemistry and physics lab with me in high school and always tried to be patient with me as he led me along at about double the pace the instructor set. We nearly blew up the school one day with an intriguing experiment using sodium and hydrochloric acid, but that is another story.

THE FABRIC OF FRIENDSHIP

Their father did everything upside down or backwards, not so much because he was stubborn, as most of his neighbors thought, but because his mind was so unceasingly curious that he could not force it into standard channels. Or at least he did not choose to.

Many of his outbuildings—the granary and hencoop, for instance—were made of big old pickle vats with roofs built on. They were odd and helped give the farmstead a quixotic appearance, but they were sturdy and serviceable and he had picked them up for practically nothing.

He had built his barn entirely out of poles and braced it with wire cable, so it was constructed more like a cage than a frame, but was solid nonetheless. As a main source of power, he converted the rear gears of a junked automobile to a sweep, and a horse walked around the circle providing power to turn a grindstone or a cement mixer or a pump. It worked perfectly, of course, but it was not conventional and added to the feeling that the man was odd. And of course we had the peasant's distrust of oddity; only a highly sophisticated community really welcomes or seeks change or the unusual, the innovative. Individuals are occasionally creative, but communities usually are not, and so his genius was largely shunted to the side, which probably suited him just as well; he could putter in peace, not much giving a damn what people thought. His farm was a laboratory in more than the usual sense. I suspect that his determination to persist in his odd ways was one of the reasons that a large portion of his many children rose out of this virtually penniless background to make important contributions as scientists, physicians, journalists. Perhaps Shaw's comment, which my eccentric neighbor never heard, applies: "The reasonable man adapts to his environment. The unreasonable man attempts to adapt his environment to him. Therefore, all progress depends on the unreasonable man." Or something like that. It was a useful lesson that I learned firsthand.

Another neighbor had a partially mad wife who spent most of her time playing classics on the piano. He used to sing arias from Wagner and Verdi as he tilled the fields. When it was his turn to feed threshers or silo fillers, the whole crew drove into town to eat at the restaurant. The yard grew up to weeds and trees, and she stayed indoors, playing the piano and listening to records and the radio. We never crept up to the house as children might, to peer in the windows or listen to the playing—not so much because we feared being caught and punished as because we were afraid that we might offend a neighbor. Since we lived together forever, one hesitated long about giving offense.

The father of one of my friends had an old Chevy that he always drove like a maniac. We loved to ride somewhere with him after dark, perhaps home from the free show, for he would crowd the old clunker up to perhaps 45 or 50 miles an hour, and then let off on the gas. We would all hang out the back window, for then he would retard the spark and the result would be a backfire which without benefit of much muffler would produce a long string of sparks to accompany the explosions. He always said he was "burning out the chimney."

THE FABRIC OF FRIENDSHIP

Some men had difficulty adapting to the new machinery, the automobiles in particular. One old man came to church regularly in a 1928 Chevy which he had bought reluctantly when his Model T Ford finally gave up the ghost. He never quite mastered the clutch and gear system, and his Sunday morning departure from church was a classic performance. He would start the engine, depress the clutch, and shift into low. He would then press the accelerator to the floor and when the engine reached its maximum revolutions, he would begin to let in the clutch a little. When the car began to move, he would suddenly release the clutch and take his foot off the gas. The car would make a tremendous lurch and shudder almost to a stop, whereupon he would depress the clutch, shift into second, open the throttle again, and jerk the car forward a few more feet. Finally he would gain enough momentum to shift into high and proceed calmly home at 15 or 20 miles an hour. All the boys of the parish would rush out of church to observe the performance, and he was affectionately known as "Old burn-em-up clutch." He was our version of "Laugh-In."

If the community had low tolerance for genius, it had plenty of room to close ranks around the unfortunate. One old man, either injured in World War I or congenitally retarded, lived in a rotting log house without heat, plumbing, or floor. He had hitched an old engine, probably salvaged from a Model T Ford, to a bench saw and made potato crates for a living. He would gather the planks of elm and ash, cut them to half-inch boards, make his corners, and sell the crates for, as I recall, 50 or 60 cents each. They were good crates, and no one around would have thought of going elsewhere to buy them. In pursuit of his livelihood, he had cut off parts of several fingers. His nickname was "Batty," but we never called him that to his face. Sometimes, he would gather up a few squash in a gunny sack and walk the mile or so to our house to make us a present. He would never accept anything in return except our patronage of his crate factory. It was generally believed that he had a small pension, and the crate business brought him $100 or $200 a year, I suppose. We thought he subsisted almost completely on sardines, for his teeth had long since rotted away. On occasion, he would tool into town in his Model T, which he kept running long past the time it became an antique. He never bought a license for it, and no one would ever have thought of ticketing him for operating it illegally. Of course, he never had a driver's license, either. The land where his old log cabin sat was owned by a neighboring farmer and there was no thought of asking him for rent. He lived out his life in his own private self-supporting dignity, and when he was found dead one day, we mourned and buried him with as much respect as anyone else in the community.

So we did another neighbor, who had not adjusted well to the tractor. When Dad first had his F-12, they had hitched it to the potato digger. As it reached the end of the row, our friend, who was driving, had begun to yell "Whoa!" When the tractor did not respond, he pulled at the reins as hard as he could, and wound up with the steering wheel in his lap and the tractor snarled in a couple of rods of wire fencing.

THE FABRIC OF FRIENDSHIP

Some of the community's favorite stories came down for generations. One was about a man who was starting his homestead, trying to clear enough land for a sustenance crop, build a log house so his family could join him in the spring, and get up some sort of shelter for the horses and cattle. He had been forced to work dawn to dark seven days a week, and the priest missed him.

One day the Father stopped by to chide his parishioner for his failure to attend mass. He began with praise, remarking again and again, "What a wonderful house you and the Lord have built"; "What a wonderful crop you and the Lord have made"; and concluding, "You and the Lord are making a wonderful farm here." The man leaned on his ax for a moment and responded, "Father, do you remember what this place looked like when the Lord was working it alone?"

Another tale I have always cherished concerned my paternal grandfather, a man with his religious convictions well in hand. He was dealing with a neighbor for a horse outside the church one morning and the bargaining had reached its climax. The last bell rang, and my grandfather put an end to the talk with his final offer as they walked into the church. "Twenty-four dollars," he said, as he dipped his hand into the holy water font, and the final words accompanied the motions where one usually says "In the name of the Father . . ." as his hand made the sign of the cross, "and not a damned cent more."

Still another favorite story came down from my maternal great-grandmother, who had a gift of acid in her tongue and passed it along to her daughters. She was an unliberated woman, married to a man who dominated her and his family and his home in a backwoods area of upper Michigan. In subsistence days, this domination was not unusual because there was little latitude for wife or children; if they did not choose to submit, and he persisted, they could not leave, for there was often simply no place to go.

The many children attended a one-room school, walking to and from it each day along a sand trail through the forest. One winter morning a blizzard raged, and my great-grandmother determined that the children should not have to go to school that day. At breakfast, they began to display a little of their enthusiasm for the unexpected holiday. Then my great-grandfather announced that, as long as they didn't have to go to school, the boys might as well come and help him in the woods. Their mother did not demur; she proceeded to help them into the layers of clothing they would need to survive the cold. But she did turn to her husband and say, "John, dear, may the dog stay in the house?"

Our family made local history the day our backhouse burned. This was not one of the more fancy backhouses. It was a plain little frame structure with a shingle roof, plaster on the inside walls, hook on the outside of the door, latch on the inside—a two-holer, unpainted, with the regulation Sears Roebuck catalog. We had put plumbing into the house some years before and by the time the backhouse burned in 1947 or 1948, it was used only in emergencies.

But then, it had never been the most popular spot on the farm. Some thousands of years ago, the now lost civilization of Crete had developed a rough form of indoor plumbing. It is not difficult to see what spurred them onward, if you have been at the mercy of an outdoor privy for a long time.

Our privy stood perhaps a hundred feet from the house, against the woodshed, and we piled junk on the near side. Once every year or so, we would pull the wagon up to the junk pile, shovel everything on, and haul it up to "the hole," a deep depression at the line fence just up the hill. On the July day when the backhouse caught fire, we had not yet hauled off the junk, and there were tin cans, broken glass, and other such things piled against it.

We were at lunch one day in July when there came a banging on the back door. I answered it, frightened beforehand because no one comes banging on doors in that country. A stranger standing there yelled that the outhouse was on fire. He had been driving by, seen the flames, and stopped to give the alarm.

Fine little flames were climbing up the side, reaching for the roof. Someone called the township fire department, and we all piled out of the house. We brought milk pails, dipped water from the stock tank 50 feet away, and splashed it over the backhouse.

We might have gotten the fire out, but it was spreading onto the floor of the woodshed, also an old tinder-dry frame building with a shingle roof. There was nothing to do but get behind the backhouse with some 2-by-4s and, in best traditions of Halloween, tip it over—frontward, away from the woodshed, where we let it burn.

In the meantime, the alarm had been sounded at the volunteer fire department. The classic scene ensued; every able-bodied man in town dropped his work to rush for the fire station. The barber would leave a client lathered if necessary, the grocery store clerk would leave change unmade, the man in the dry goods store would leave a customer with one shoe off.

Something more than civic responsibility spurred these men to run to the fire house. The first one there got to drive the truck, which, given the excitement of the event and the infrequency of its occurrence, was no small diversion.

That is, he got to drive it if they could get it started. The old hulk might sit for months undriven, and the battery was likely to be down. When enough men gathered, though, they could give it a push and it would roll down the driveway and might start by engaging the gears and turning the motor over. On this day, they got the truck started one way or another and headed out for our farm, a little more than two miles distant.

The progress of the fire fighters was always a spectacle. Fires were uncommon and any excitement was always welcome. Also, it was pretty much understood that there was virtually no chance of the equipment's standing up to a fire of any size; if it was a real fire in a house or barn, you could be fairly well assured that the place would burn to the ground. So a caravan of cars always followed the fire truck. If the location of the fire was common knowledge, the cars would pass the truck. This was not difficult, because the truck had a maximum speed of about 35 on a slight downhill grade.

THE FABRIC OF FRIENDSHIP

The low top speed of the truck introduced another factor; some auxiliary power was desirable. There was only one man who always had a reliable and fairly new car—the postman, who drove the rural route daily. He had a priority and always could buy a new car. He could afford it, too, for he had a mileage allowance. Right after the war, he bought a new 1946 Studebaker, and on the day of our fire, he had a new Mercury. If he was around at the time of the fire, it was his duty to pull up behind the truck, nose the front bumper of his car against its wooden rear bumper, and then push his accelerator to the floor, pushing the truck to higher speeds. With the mailman pushing, it could sometimes make 40 or 45 miles an hour.

The spectacle was improved that pleasant July day because the last time the truck was used had been in the winter and the snow chains were still attached to the rear wheels. Down the gravel road they came, truck wide open, mailman pushing at the rear, sparks flying from the tire chains, siren wailing, half a dozen cars trailing along behind, cheering them on.

Of course by the time they had gone through all this and arrived at the farm, we had tipped the backhouse over and given up any attempt to put out the fire. But the truck pulled up as close as it could, a hose was dipped into the stock tank, and the pumper started. The hose leaked badly, and the pressure didn't amount to much, so the effect was about that of a leaky garden hose spouting out a puny stream of water. As long as the stock tank held out, that is; when that went dry in a few minutes, the value of the fire truck came to an end.

Nevertheless, they were able to get enough water onto the fire so that they saved the ends of several boards and we had to haul them up to the hole the next day. Had they not come at all, we would have been saved some work.

Everyone stood around after it was all over, reluctant to end the excitement. Someone took off the tire chains, or at least what was left of them after the battering. The postman resumed his route, and after a while the truck went back to the fire house. There was a scorched spot on the woodshed shingles ever after, the backhouse was gone for good, and we had to find a new place to pile junk. We finally decided that sun reflecting from a bit of broken glass had started the blaze.

The bitter days of the depression provided their own crop of stories. It was said that a census taker from Washington came by a farm once to ask some questions and found the farmer milking his only cow. The man asked his visitor to wait until he had finished with the cow. Presently, he stood up, drank deeply of the milk in the pail, then he walked over and poured some into a cat dish. He sloshed the rest around in the pail, threw it out, and hung the pail upside down on a nail. "There," he told his visitor, "the chores are finished, supper's over, and the dishes are washed. What can I do for you?"

Somewhere the notion has developed that farmers are silent people, inarticulate with each other. I did not observe this in my childhood. We were a gabby family; we talked a lot, and sometimes we argued; we were noisy, and we whooped up the card games at night so it was a wonder the younger ones ever got any sleep. Yet my father was not articulate with his children. We speak with him still on his own terms, no matter how far any of us has gone. For we went away, we changed, and when we go back, he is the same. He has his place, after all, and whatever we might ever laugh about, it has never occurred to any of us to laugh at that.

We remember, I think, one of the best stories he ever told us. Late one spring day, a family with their belongings in their wagon and their stock in tow stopped by a farm and asked if they could camp in the orchard overnight. The favor readily granted, they staked out their horses and cattle and started a cook fire. Late in the evening, their host strolled down to see if everything was all right, and to pick up any news they might have. The transient fell to talking.

"We sure hope we find better neighbors where we're headed than those we left behind," he said. "They were awful people; unhelpful, spiteful, nasty. We could hardly wait to get away, and we hope we find better ahead."

"You won't," the farmer said.

In the fall, another family on the move camped in the orchard. As the farmer talked with them that evening, the conversation was different. "We hated to leave our neighbors behind," the man said. "They were helpful, really wonderful folks. We hope we'll find people as nice where we're going."

"You will," the farmer said.

5. LIVESTOCK

I once had a cow who was retarded. It was not her fault; she had as good upbringing as the next cow, and I knew her mother, who was bright enough. She was a registered Jersey, and in our passion to breed into her an extraordinary capacity to produce milk, we had allowed her to be shortchanged somewhere in the brains department.

For the most part, she got along quite well, content to hang back, take the lowest rung on the social ladder, wait until all the other cows had gone into the barn and slip in last, even then a little uncertain that the lone remaining stanchion was her place. She was friendly and would come up to me in the barnyard to have her head scratched, but she always behaved as though she wasn't sure whether I was me or my father.

Her first calf confused her. Her motherly instincts were uncertain; one moment, she would bawl for the calf, and the next she would drift over to stand staring in a puzzled fashion at the barn wall as though she had forgotten where she was. She learned to allow herself to be milked fairly easily, but she would regress now and then and have to be gently reminded that we had been through this before and she really did know all about it. Sometimes, she would be chewing her cud in a kind of daze and would wake up when the milking was half finished and jump around in amazement or even try to kick off the milker.

She was right-handed, like all our cows, because we trained them to be milked from the right side, but once in a while she would notice someone milking the cow to her left, be seized with the fear that he was about to approach her improperly and go rigid.

She was afraid of the dog, although the other cows came to realize quickly that they and the dog were in things together. They would allow the dog to preserve his dignity by appearing to herd them to the barn, but they really did not fear him and they let him sleep with them in the winter. Not my little cow. If she spied him out of the corner of her eye, her nervous system would snap shut the milk veins and we would have to wait until she had calmed down before we could milk her. A hayfork out of place might set her off, or an unexpected cat or a slammed door.

Her first year's production was high enough to justify

considerable patience, or so I thought. My father was not so sure. When I left the farm for college, she didn't last long. He mumbled something about her not breeding, but I have always had a lingering suspicion that he shipped her because she pressed too hard on his patience.

Cattle have more personality than is usually recognized, and in those days of small herds there was a strong bond between the owner and his cattle. Partly it grew out of memories of the times when men and cows needed each other so desperately, when they served as beasts of burden as well as giving a little milk to keep the children healthy; partly it was because they are fully domesticated, really unable to fend for themselves, and as such are, like children, a burden that fills for the farmer some of the need to be needed. The land is neutral to you; you can leave it and it will revert to its natural ways. But the dairy cow can no longer do without the herdsman. We have bred her so she is no longer self-sufficient, and so we must care for her.

Years back, the farmers in that area kept cattle that they called simply "red cows." They were big shaggy beasts, graded down slightly from the breed developed in Durham County, England, which has evolved into Milking Shorthorns. They were proper cattle for a new area. Like the resourceful farm wives, they could pretty much do for themselves. They could range around through the swamps and woods, foraging for themselves, make it through the winter on whatever was at hand. Their long coats recalled the mammoths that roamed the land with men thousands of years ago, and part of our fondness may have come from a vestige of a forgotten memory.

LIVESTOCK

Despite their name, they were not all red. Some had flecks of white to make a lovely roan color, and some were nearly all white.

Memories about them tend to be selective, and they probably come off the better for it. My father recalled that they all gave a pail of milk twice a day when fresh. Perhaps they did; it was customary to have them drop their calves in the spring so that the flow of milk, naturally highest right after calving, would be encouraged further by the rich new pasture. Nearly any big cow would give milk copiously under those conditions. They were pretty much dry by fall, and the shipments to the creamery dropped off dramatically in winter.

As the butter market improved and it became apparent that the cooperative creamery could sell all it could make, farmers looked to more productive breeds, cows bred especially for milk and particularly for milk high in butterfat content. Cream was the main goal; skim milk only a useful by-product.

Sometimes by intent, sometimes by accident, the herds were converted from the red cows to dairy breeds. Jerseys were much favored because they give milk with the highest butterfat of all—around 6 percent. They are hardy grazers, docile, and easy to care for. Developed on the Isle of Jersey in the English Channel, they are among the most efficient breeds in the world at converting grass to milk. Smaller than shorthorns, they weigh 1,000 pounds or less fully grown, yet even in those days they would produce 5,000 pounds of 6 percent milk in ten months. They also helped break the seasonal cycle of the dairy operation.

Good farmers bred them so that most calves came in the fall, but ideally the calving was spaced all year round. The natural surge of milk production would be encouraged with grain and protein supplements through the winter, and a "second freshening" would come in the spring when they were turned out to the new pasture.

A few farmers went in for the bigger Holsteins, but the Jersey breeders said the big black-and-white cows gave skim milk. In fact, it tested only 3.5 percent and was stark white in comparison to the creamy yellow Jersey product. Holsteins are nearly half again as large as Jerseys and require terrific quantites of roughage, as do the Shorthorns. Their supporters claimed that the difference was more than made up by the value of the cows when sold for beef at the conclusion of their dairy career, and the greater value of the calves when sold for veal.

Such matters are not conjectural now, when record keeping and cost accounting have become as efficient on prosperous farms as in any other business. But before the influence of the state agricultural college seeped into the central part of Michigan, the disagreements could not be resolved by facts and were the stuff of long arguments over the tables in the beer garden downtown, when the old farmers played solo or pinochle or later euchre on long winter days.

Whatever the breed, cows and herds retain their personality and order. There is a fairly rigid social structure, for instance, similar to the pecking order noted among chickens. Sociologists have long noted that one particular hen can peck all others, one hen in a flock can peck no other hens but all can peck her, and the rest fall into a range between. I have no idea why anyone would study chickens rather than cows, but the same feature exists among cattle, though it is not widely noted.

In the summer, the herd was turned out to graze between milkings and when called or herded up by a boy and his dog, the cows formed in a single line to march toward the barn. The order of appearance in this line was fixed. The reigning cow was always in first place, the others taking their turn in line, down to the young heifers who brought up the rear. The young were quickly taught by butting, or with the horns if these had not been taken off, where their place was—at the back of the bus, figuratively.

When they reached the barn, each took her own stanchion. If an unwary new addition to the herd tried to take the stanchion claimed by an older cow, mayhem would result. A fight would break out immediately, with the herdsman in the middle, trying to get things straightened out before the brawl spread through the herd.

Cows are captives of habit, and such a disruption would throw confusion into all of them. Sometimes the only solution would be to drive them all out of the barn and start over, hopefully with the new cow held out so she could come in and take the place left for her when the others had been stanchioned.

Dogs were quick to note this trait and learned to pick up the herd leader and start her toward the barn. The others would follow. Should she take it in her head to come to the barn unbidden, the others followed her lead, trailing along, chewing their cuds, happy to be told what to do. Once established, these patterns were broken only at calving time, when the mother wanted privacy and would slip away to the woods or any cover she could find, even breaking a fence on occasion to hide with her new calf.

A frightened cow is simply unmanageable. She will run through a barbed wire fence as though crazy or take off on a long charge across a field, udder swinging crazily, sometimes spraying the milk from the swinging teats. The udders are vulnerable and sensitive, but an alarmed cow will plunge through barbed wire, cutting her udder and teats and putting a hellish burden of careful treatment on the hands of the herdsman. If a cow cuts a teat while she is in heavy production, the milk must be taken out even though any pressure on the teat is painful. The job can require considerable patient negotiation.

Odd things can set cows off. They may graze quietly through a drenching rain, but if the herd leader becomes excited, she may ring her tail over her back and take off for the far corner of the field, the rest running frantically along. A strange dog may scare them, but on many occasions, I have found them joined in the pasture by two or three deer, all happily coexisting on the green grass.

Cats hang around barns, hoping for warm milk. Now and then, a lusty old tom will show up, looking for something else. He might stroll innocently enough down the planks that form the top of the stanchion row; if one of the cows spots him, the whole herd might panic.

Big as they are, cows are subject to an awesome variety of diseases, most of them connected to milk production. The cycle begins with calving, which generates the natural urge to produce milk. While they will manage the birth alone most of the time, some complication is not unusual. One difficulty is inability to give birth, with prolonged and fruitless labor. This is sometimes hard to notice, for the cow cannot speak of her problem, and even good records will not show the exact day she should have her calf. The careful herdsman keeps an eye on her, checking the progress of the calf by gently bumping her side. By the fourth or fifth month of the nine-month pregnancy, you can usually find the calf's head. When the time draws near, a careful eye will tell if she is in difficulty. Nowadays, a veterinarian is called to help, but when I was a boy his calls were too costly except in cases of major emergency, and we tried to help a cow give birth ourselves. If she is in pain, and trusts you, she will let you reach in, find the calf, perhaps straighten it out so it will exit in the normal way. On occasion, a vet must be called to kill and take out the unborn calf in order to save the cow.

Fairly frequently, a cow has difficulty in discharging the placenta and must have help. This is not one of the farmer's favorite tasks.

But if all goes well, the proud mother will lick her little baby dry and make only token protest when it is taken from her. It is best to have them out of sight of each other, or she will counsel the calf against cooperation, and it must be taught to drink out of a pail when its instinct is to suck.

For the first few days after a cow freshens, the milk is more suited for calf food than for humans. What the calf cannot drink must be thrown away until the milk returns to its regular composition.

Teaching a calf to drink can be a painful process. The

idea is to take some milk in a pail, dip your fingers in it, let the calf suck your fingers—hopefully with as little chewing as possible—and then draw him down to the level of the milk so he will turn to drinking.

Smart calves learn this in a lesson or two, but some just can't get it figured out. They may butt the pail out of your hands, or bite, and as they get hungry they bawl. Then their mother bawls back if she is around, and the whole affair becomes unpleasant for everyone. One day after an unsuccessful third or fourth attempt to get a calf to drink, my oldest brother proclaimed in anger that he was going to let the calf starve and tell God it died.

Care of a dairy herd is an endless task and can take as much time as the herdsman wants to spend. But it develops a healthy affection between herdsman and herd. City people generally find the odor in a barn unpleasant. When I left to go to college I became so lonesome for it on occasion that I had to hike out to the college dairy barn to assuage my longings.

This pertains, of course, to the old way of dairying. Now the cows are run loose in sheds, handled only at milking time when they pass through a glass-and-steel milking parlor, receiving a ration of grain in exchange for 12 hours of milk production. They are identified by numbers on tags around their neck rather than by name. It is more efficient, but more impersonal, and I would not care to run a herd in the modern way.

Pride and pain come in unpredictable doses from dairy herd management. When we began testing, we found that our herd was among the highest-producing in the area. Although our cows were not registered, my father even sold an occasional bull calf to another farmer for breeding. There is pride in knowing that a particular cow is the result of careful selection and breeding, and the dairyman can often remember for two or three generations the genealogy of every cow in his herd. By then there is more to it than money.

But death can come quickly. A cow can pick up a piece of metal—a nail, a bit of wire, a fragment of a broken farm implement—and swallow it down, not noticing that it is not grass. If it is not picked off in the reticulum, a natural screening point in such cases, it can puncture an intestine. Only the most valuable cow warrants the kind of expensive surgery that would save her, and a producer worth $500 one day can be dead the next. The owner stands by helpless. It is a nice time to believe in God.

My father made the switch from the old red Shorthorns to Guernseys under duress, abruptly. In the annual testing for brucellosis (Bang's disease) one year in the 1930s, we found a "positive." Under law, this meant the disposal of the herd. The cows were shipped and sold for beef, the barn was scrubbed and disinfected and cleaned, and we were ready to start over. The trauma is not much less than that of, say, a barn's burning, though given the value of the diseased animals as beef—the meat is not tainted—the financial shock is eased a little.

For various reasons, one no doubt being that Guernsey cows weighed less than Shorthorns and so could be bought for less, my father restocked with good-quality Guernseys.

Their arrival is imprinted on my mind. After becoming

accustomed to cows as big shaggy red critters, I can recall these elegant, almost dainty by comparison, fawn-and-white spotted cows coming down the tailgate from the big truck. Guernseys have long faces, intelligent eyes and ears, and they picked their way around the yard, sniffing, trying to identify something familiar. We children stood around, trying to be friendly, welcoming them, making them at home as best we could.

I wonder what the parallel event would be in city life. Perhaps the closest thing would be the arrival of a large new family in a highly stable small neighborhood, and their greeting by an aggressively friendly contingent of other children. We knew that these cows were to be part of our lives, that our future prosperity depended to a great extent on them, that much of our time would be spent with them, that they would determine our schedules, be important sights on the landscape of our farm, and that we would get to know them all as individuals.

We busied ourselves with naming them, Dad being particularly patient and generally accepting our names without argument. Molly became the herd leader, Daisy the high producer who gave us generation after generation of heifers, all of them docile and productive, well mannered and intelligent. Daisy was the kind of cow that herds are built around, and her calving was an annual event for years—would she drop a bull or a heifer? We were like Chinese in reverse, wanting a heifer so she would produce a calf and milk, scorning bulls because they are of slight value save for veal or an occasional sale for breeding stock.

LIVESTOCK

Dairy cows determined much of the cropping system and thus the seasonal work; they made the major impact on the way a farm looked, too.

Everyone knows the classic dairy farm scene—the big white or red barn, the silos, perhaps a board fence around the farmyard. The scene is different today, of course, with the steel-roofed loafing pen and the pole barn replacing the big structure, contributing to efficiency and bringing an end to beauty, as a subdivision of factory-built houses gives shelter to more people but cannot match the appeal of old-fashioned houses built by a carpenter one by one for the people who were to live in them. The old dairy barns were the expression of a man's dreams, the new one-story sheds the expression of an efficient economic decision. We do not put pictures of loafing pens on calendars.

But the visual impact of a dairy herd is more pervasive than that. To begin with, all the parts of the farm where they range—in days past, that meant the entire acreage —must be fenced. The stump fences took up too much space, shaded crops on both sides, and as a result were uneconomical. They were first replaced with barbed-wire fences strung on cedar posts. The life of a cedar fence post is five or ten years, and when we had the money, we replaced these with steel posts, which last two or three times as long. Still later, we supplemented the fencing between fields in the interior of the farm with electric fences— temporary barriers that took little or no space, did not make for lost cropland because they could be moved from year to year, and enabled rotational grazing. The electricity was provided by little battery-powered fencers, which gave a mild shock to any cow that touched them. The cattle learned quickly to respect electric fences.

Nothing decorates a farm like a herd of grazing cattle. They spread across a field in their search for grass; they lie down together in a shady place while they chew their cuds and digest the grass. But, best, they form long single files going to the field or coming home to be milked. Strolling along at the pace of a slow walk, they represent prosperity, and permanence, and continuity. They are soil-conserving income producers, and none are more beautiful than Guernseys, fawn and white against the green and gold of nature, pastoral pastels with vivid backgrounds, a motif in motion.

Yet most farmers come to hate cows sooner or later. They are hard masters while they are beautiful mistresses. Each morning and night, they must be cared for, their milk taken, their needs met as they met ours. In the winter manure must be removed, stalls cleaned, mangers swept, hay and silage hauled down and measured out, grain ground and mixed with protein supplements, doled out according to production needs.

They drool into their mangers, and occasional cleaning is needed to keep away the sour smells. Calves must be broken to drink, cows broken to milk. Their sexual needs are converted to the needs of the farmer and must be attended to, and careful records kept. Their milk must be measured and tested to see if they are producing satisfactorily. Horns must be cut off when they are calves, so they do not gouge one another as adults. The herdsman usually wears rubber boots of some sort in the barn, and these should be washed before entering and upon leaving to prevent the spread of disease.

Their marvelous milk, promoted as nature's most nearly perfect food, is highly delicate. If not cooled quickly, it sours. All the milking utensils must be cleaned as carefully as the plates and forks of a restaurant; the cooler where the milk is kept must be sterile and clean.

When the cows first freshen, their milk, designed by nature for the nourishment of their calves, though rich and good, smells bad and is even more subject to souring than normal milk. A fresh cow may bloat if she gets too much sweet grass; she will blow up like a balloon, perhaps fall over in the field, and her side must be punctured to let the gas out.

Heavy milk production may lead to "milk fever," an illness generated by the tremendous changes in body chemistry that accompany this sudden outpouring of milk. If the cow is infected by mastitis the milk may clot in the udder and must then be thrown away until the infection is cleared up. Ideally, cows should live in a hospital or a sterile environment like that in which space vehicles are assembled. The problem of providing a hospital for patients who roam the open fields most of the time is a chronic challenge to the dairyman and is one of the reasons so many have switched to the confinement of the loafing pen and yard.

They are subject to parasites and internal disorders, and they cannot speak of their difficulties. Only highly prosperous farms can afford the regular visits of a veterinarian, and many cows simply waste away and are shipped for cheap beef because the dairyman did not know what was wrong with them and could not afford to find out.

Eventually, the round of chores becomes a burden, a routine that destroys the spontaneity of life. The farmer who could not afford the help to get away for a vacation would come, through the years, to regard himself as a slave to the dairy barn. For the milker, there are no weekends, no sick days, no time for carelessness.

The whole round of work became so onerous for those unable to break away from it now and then that they would come to neglect the cows, to manufacture reasons for dispersing the herd and turning to crop farming. Modern concentrations of dairy operations are in part a reaction to this need for constant care. In a factory operation, the work can be shared; there can be vacations, time off. Even the keeper of an art museum wants time away from his paintings, a change in surroundings, a shift in pace and occupation; the scientist wants to read detective stories or science fiction; the teacher likes a summer of physical work. For the dairy farmer the organization had to be changed to meet his human needs. Like so many changes we make, this one went too far, and we will probably some day manufacture milk artificially. Ecologically, that may be wrong; in terms of man's relationship to his environment, it surely will be. There was too much relationship to the dairy cow, too close a bond between man and land and cow and product. We may manufacture a substitute for cows' milk, but I doubt we will be able to manufacture a replacement for the fullness of that life at its best.

Hogs are another matter.

They were consumers of our by-product, skim milk. They required less care, for hogs are by nature more hardy than cows, cleaner, more able to care for themselves. But, perhaps because they were less dependent, we never liked them much.

Big white hogs dominated the farms a century ago. The idea was to get huge quantities of pork—a little ham but lots of bacon and lard and salt pork. These low-grade foods balanced diets, filled a need. As the nation grew more prosperous, the demand for lean pork grew. We bred lean hogs. In high school, I converted our swine herd to registered Duroc Jersey, then noted for its ability to make lean market hogs that would command higher prices. They were all-red pigs, and we tended them carefully with heat lamps in their pens at farrowing time. But the hogs, like the chickens, we let go without regret when the time came to convert to the sale of grade A whole milk. Hogs are, finally, a commodity, dairy cows a way of life.

One of my most pleasant adventures in cattle keeping began and ended in the dust and roar of a county fairground. A feature of the fair in those days was the calf scramble. Sponsors would buy a herd of wild range steer calves, perhaps thirty or forty of them. These would be loosed in a big pen in front of the grandstand for an evening event.

Boys who lived in the county would sign up to catch them. As a member of the Future Farmers of America and a student of agriculture, with no intention of ever doing anything but farm, I naturally entered the competition. I was also a skinny 130 pounds at age fifteen, tough as a nail but not much thicker than one. The object was to catch a calf, throwing the loop around his nose and then making a turn around his neck—it was not legal to subdue the calves by throttling them—and hauling him up to the rail to tie him down. The successful boy kept the calf through the year, returning him to show and auction at the next fair.

Each boy received a rope some 6 feet long with a loop knitted into the end. We lined up along the fence and at a given signal gave chase to the calves, who huddled in terror in the far corner. It was a glorious, post-gladiatorial contest, unequal on both sides. I caught one of the larger calves; he outweighed me four to one. But somehow I secured him to the rail and gained possession of him.

He came home with us in a trailer that night. We unloaded him at the hog pen, crowded him through the door, and tied him, terrified and lowing, to an old potato digger parked in the corner.

I named him Jiggs, and for days, I worked with him to gain his confidence. In a month, he would come to me, welcome his halter, and we would walk together around the yard. He spent the year in splendor, with his own box stall, all the fine corn and oats he could eat, gaining 2 pounds a day, growing with incredible speed into a fat show steer.

In the spring, he weighed nearly a half a ton and was the object of almost constant attention. I taught him to stand long, showing off his magnificent fat. The white switch on his tail was backcombed and teased until it would stand out in a spray bigger than a milk pail. I polished his hoofs with linseed oil and wetted his sides and combed them into loops and swirls. He became obsessively fond of me and would stand in the barn, looking over the half door, bawling irritably if I left to go to town. When I got back, there he would be, bawling like a spoiled kid, the silky white coat of his pendulous dewlap hanging over the door.

A day or two before fair time, he broke out of the barn one night and went to graze with the cows. I was furious at him: contact with fresh grass might upset the delicate fattening diet. But he did not get very sick and was shiny and clean by fair day.

Through the year, we took tours of the scramble calves, big caravans of boys and fathers and friends and agriculture teachers tearing around the county, trying to visit all forty calves in a day or a day and a half. We checked feeds and growth, gauging growth by means of a tape with the girth measures indicated in approximate weight, which was wrapped around the calf. The records were checked, too, and the progress in training the calves.

Some of the calves had a low-producing dairy cow assigned to them for the year as a nurse. These calves had a glossy coat and a layer of fat that made the rest of us feel as though our calves would be outclassed, but we knew that the cost records would show the growth as incredibly expensive.

When we went to the fair, my Jiggs waddled along with me without a halter, heeling like a dog as I exercised him down the fairway early in the morning before the crowds arrived. The carnival folk hated to see us come, for the calves—fat, lumbering critters weighing 1,100 and 1,200 pounds by then—would defecate copiously on the tan-bark, causing the swearing roustabouts to dash out with shovels and brooms to clean up the piles before the customers got there. We slept beside the calves on the straw, feeding them by hand and watering them with pails, grooming and preening them almost beyond reason.

And then came the night of the show, when they were judged before the crowded grandstands. The test of the year's work . . . would the calves bolt in excitement before those jammed grandstands, those shouts and cries, those bright lights? We walked in single file, swinging off to face the stands, moving the calves' feet into position with our training sticks. Jiggs stood there dozing, nuzzling me now and then for reassurance, chewing his cud, obese and lazy and oblivious to everything but the grabs of the judges checking the thickness of flanks and rump.

He won second for fat and form; I won fourth for over-all performance—my records, his weight gain and composition, my showmanship. Then he was auctioned off, bringing some $44 a hundred, $540 for 1,240 pounds. Out of that, I paid his original cost—about $165 for his purchase as a feeder a year earlier, a wild calf of 500 pounds shipped in from the West at $33 a hundred, and paid my father for the feed he had consumed in the year. The remainder was to be seed money for purchase of other cattle.

After it was all over, I let him wear the big pink ribbon back to the shed. I went out with friends, walking over to the little county seat for a thrill, which probably included a 1 o'clock breakfast in an all-night eatery along the highway.

The buyer came to get Jiggs early the next morning. We had slept together again, and we smelled of each other. I gave him a last drink, groomed him head to tail, even wiping the moisture from around his big eyes. He watched me carefully and butted me a little when I hugged his massive white head. The buyer came, backing his truck as close as he could to the tent. He had to lead Jiggs out himself, and the big steer balked, wondering why I didn't help. I couldn't even watch. It was a bittersweet relief when finally he was gone.

The dairy cattle are gone from the area now, too. When I rode my bike to town as a boy, there were six big herds, counting my father's, along the two miles. Besides our Guernseys, there were two herds of Jerseys and three of Holsteins. Our cows have long since been sold. One of the Jersey herds remains, and one of the Holsteins. That is above average for the area. The barns are empty, and the grass grows in the barnyard fence rows. The places look a little shaggy, as though something that belongs there has vanished.

6. WOODS

Our most important woods, spiritually and economically, were maple and elm. Earlier, and especially farther north, it had been the pine—that great white magnet that drew men and money to the north woods, dominating the landscape, the legends, and the lives. But nature had been too generous with the pine. Like the giant sequoia, it was too well adapted to the uses of men and so it was harvested, cut down, reaped, and finally ravaged from the country so that it is now remembered mainly in histories and in a state park.

Not so the maple. Harder wood, it was not so prone to pillage. More will and muscle were needed to turn it to man's purposes, and so it survived longer. Nor was there as much of it. The pines stood bough to bough from one horizon to the next, inviting pillage like the buffalo, an irresistible invitation to men with a sense for mass production, with a will to build and develop, an urge to prosper as mightily as the forests grew. The pines yielded up their bounty, a massive harvest that could not be repeated. But the maple was a more solitary tree. It shared space with elms and evergreens, oaks and hickory and ash and beech, some cherry and walnut. A maple might be a cordial neighbor to a cluster of birch, might even stand alone on a knob of clay, watching over the sand flats, giving the deer a spot of shade as they paused on their way to a new browse, making a place for the birds.

In the early days the barns and houses and sheds were built of pine, mostly cut on our own farms. And what pines they must have been! My father's barn is 36 by 50 feet with an overchute—an extension of the second story over one side to provide a small shelter for the cattle. The entire barn is framed and sheathed with pine cut on those acres. The main beams are 50 feet long, hewn by hand, almost knotless the whole length, 12 to 16 inches square. The beams were notched by masters of a craft now extinct, drilled to take wooden nails carved out on the site, and pieced together like a giant puzzle to be assembled and hoisted into place by horses and fixed with the wooden pegs, a mighty cathedral to the dreams of the men who built them.

But by the time my father bought his place the pines were gone, and we turned to the other trees for our needs.

His property had a fringe of woods along the back, edging the farm like the ring of hair clinging to the scalp of a man who is nearly bald. It joined another patch of woods at the rear of farms that backed up to ours, so there was a stretch of woods a mile long across the entire section of land, and it resumed again at both ends on the other sides of the roads. It was wide enough that none of us ever walked through it to come out the other side, yet we never called it a forest—always the woods. For a time, I wondered why. My ancestors were German, after all, and theirs is a land famous for its forests. Yet I came to realize that the word "woods" had a feudal ring to it: it was the plot of trees from which a landowner took certain necessities, and its ownership and maintenance were important in the struggle for survival and the reach toward comfort.

Our woods did not provide us with much lumber, for our building was mostly complete. We did build one shed when I was a boy, but I doubt that we needed half a dozen trees for it. But the woods provided firewood to heat the house and cook the meals. The maples yielded syrup for pancakes and now and then a wedge of sugar. The woods provided shelter for deer that we did not hunt, and a place to be alone in a spot that man visited but did not dominate. They gave us a goal for walking. When there was a confidence to be shared, a companionship to be nourished, a special time to spend with someone, it was always a good idea to take a walk to the woods. Back through the lane, half a mile to the place where the cropland gave way to the trees, we could follow a trail, kept open through the trees in the winter by horses and tractors, where we hauled out the buzz poles that would be cut into short lengths for stove wood. Or we could climb a steep little hill, hardly more than a big mound, and sit sideways while we talked, on one side the depths of the forest, on the other the open land rolling up to the buildings.

Often we saw deer. Once, when I was not yet old enough for school, we found a fawn there in the leaves at the edge of the wood. It was a soft, frail little thing, and we picked it up and took pictures of each other holding it. My mother said it weighed less than a 10-pound bag of sugar she had handled that morning. A teacher of agriculture warned us that once we had handled it and tainted it with our scent, the mother would have no more to do with the baby and it would be left to starve. The younger children half hoped so, for then we could take it to the house, nurse it with bottles of milk, and raise it for a pet. So we rushed back to the woods the next morning, or perhaps even that evening, and found the place where the leaves and grass were pressed down, but the fawn was gone, taken back by its mother to be with its own. As children, we were oddly disappointed, feeling vaguely that something had been taken from us. Now we know that something had been given us—a chance to spend a few minutes with a creature altogether natural, something soft and real, something that was then taken back to the bosom of the woods for proper care. For a few years, we used to talk about how one day the grown deer would come back out to us, like Androcles's lion, and perhaps show off a fawn of its own, share some petting, and then go back home. Of course it was a Disney fantasy, and it never happened, but it moved us a little closer to the woods.

On a businesslike basis, the woods were a source of fuel. We had to compromise, taking elms mostly, for we hoped the maples would grow into timber marketable for cash. The elms, long before they were stricken with the fatal disease that is patiently eliminating them from Michigan and elsewhere, were wonderful and stately shade trees in the cities and towns. I now live on an Elm Street, and it is clearly named for a magnificent specimen at the head of the street, perhaps the largest elm I have ever seen. It must be 30 feet to the first branch, and the great inverted pear shape reaches up 125 feet or more.

We watch the tree with fear and speculation now, hoping each spring that it will green out again, another year of grace before the cancer of Dutch elm disease infiltrates its circulatory system and strangles it to death. I do not envy the foresters when they need, finally, to climb up and take down this stately giant, branch and limb, twig and trunk.

My father's woods are dotted with dead hulks, great black skeletons that have succumbed to the illness and stand still erect but rotting. If we needed firewood, they would be ideal, for they would be dry and seasoned when cut, a quick and easy fire. But the farmhouse is heated with natural gas now, and the old wood range has been gone for a quarter-century. So the elms are not needed, and they wait, along with the obsolete old farm machinery rusting in fence corners, to rot down and rejoin the earth.

What we remember is what wretched things the elm trunks were to split for firewood, how the tangled grain defied our muscles, but how hot the chunks burned, and how they would hold a fire all night and warm the house while we slept.

The grain and fiber of wood, for a farm boy, is not a curiosity on a laboratory slide, not simply a texture to be admired in a piece of polished furniture. It becomes, through hours of sawing and splitting, an extension of his own nervous system, a part of his own muscle structure, a maze to be felt and understood.

The elm chunks were tough and sinewy, knotted twists of fiber knitted together like the shoulder muscles of a strong old horse. The limbs and trunks were hauled in pole lengths to a huge pile by the woodshed to be cut by the buzz saw into lengths that would fit into the stoves. Those pieces too large to go through the doors or to lie in the fire-pits had to be split. The splitting also opened the inside to the air, so the wood would dry sooner, burn easier.

Every stick of elm was a challenge. We would lift the chunk to the chopping block, then walk around it for a careful appraisal. Splitting was done with big double-bitted axes, dull so they would follow the grain instead of cutting it. Most of the heavy splitting axes had notches broken from the middle of the cutting bit. That meant that the ax had been struck on a rock or bit of iron one day and was no longer fit for trimming or chopping, but the notches did not harm them for splitting.

FROM THE LAND AND BACK

By looking carefully at the block of wood, the splitter could see where the grain was smoothest and attack the block there. Perhaps a corner could be popped off, sometimes the block could be divided by the ax into two or three parts so it could dry and burn. Sometimes wedges were needed where the fibers were so tangled that no ax could tear them apart.

Years later, when I read that Michelangelo would look at a piece of rough marble and see inside it the statue that he wanted to carve, I knew exactly how he felt, for that is how we looked at the blocks of wood, seeing the shape that was held inside them, looking for the statue that we would carve from them with our axes.

One gains a great respect for a piece of wood which rejects the ax, which even fights the wedges. I can remember time and again my strong father striking repeated blows of the heavy ax on a chunk of elm and seeing the ax simply bounce off as though the wood were possessed by demons.

Of course we could always win if we spent enough effort. At worst, a mark could be made with the ax, a wedge or two or three started, and sufficient battering with a sledge would finally split the chunk. And yet I can remember driving wedges so deep into the wood that they could not be extracted and still the chunk would not open. I have driven them completely through and out the other side of a chunk of elm and left the block unbroken. I have been forced to call on my father for help, and we would chop the wedges out with an ax, sometimes putting a new nick on the ax in the process. The contest would become highly personal, a man's strength and skill and tools and

determination against the twisted knots of elm. And sometimes the wood would win. The first few blocks we found
especially reluctant would make good chopping blocks.
But around any woodyard where elms were split, there
will be a chunk or two in the corner, blocks abandoned by
the splitter, small victories for nature.

Maple was a different matter. The grain was smooth and
straight, the wood white and smooth and vulnerable as a
woman's thighs. If the woodpile had many maple chunks,
my father might walk around it for an hour, simply striking the blocks where they lay, marking them. We boys
would then pick them up, perch them on the chopping
block, and give them a whack with the ax. Often a single
blow would split one into three or four parts, the breaks
already begun by my father's skilled blows. And the wood
dried quickly, burned with a fine hard heat, warmed our
house as it warmed our bodies when we split it.

Birch also split easily, as did the occasional pines that we
knocked down to form a clearing or to open up a space for
a maple to grow unchallenged. On that kind of wood a
boy learned how to split. But birch and pine are soft and
open; they burn quickly and do not hold a fire. They are
kindling woods, used only to help start the harder blocks
that gave the real heat.

The maples had a by-product too. In the early spring, as
soon as the freeze was broken and the sap began to run up
from the roots to make the maples leaf and blossom, we
would tap a dozen or two trees. We would approach the
tree with a big hand-held brace and bit, a thing shaped like
a crankshaft with a pad at the back. Butting against the

tree as though to attack it sexually, we would ram the bit into the bark and turn it, leaning our weight against the tree, driving the bit through the dry bark and the soft outer layers of wood. Four or five inches into the tree, the hymen would rupture and the sap would begin to run out. We would drive a tap into the scar—hand-carved plugs with holes forced through them and notches to hold pails. The pails would fill overnight—sometimes twice a day —and we would gather the sap into cream cans carried on planks stuck into the drawbar of the tractor. The sap would be boiled down, moisture evaporating until only the sweet syrup was left, to be filtered and strained and canned and prized for the marvelous taste it gave to pancakes. If it were boiled again, it could be reduced to sugar, an incredibly sweet treat requiring gallons and gallons of sap for a few ounces of candy.

Our palms and fingertips and our arm and shoulder and back muscles came to know the woods and trees through the antenna of sawteeth. Many people talk about chopping down trees, but in fact few are chopped down— they were and are sawed down. Now there are vicious chain saws, furious things driven by gasoline engines, rows of tiny chisels that tear the wood to shreds. But then the work was done by two men and a crosscut saw, a gentle engine of a very personal nature.

To fell a tree, a man first appraised it. When he determined that it would naturally lean in a particular direction, a notch was cut in that side of the truck to encourage the tree to topple in a predictable way. The sharp bright double-bitted axes did that job. Then came the saw—a long ribbon of flexible steel, with great teeth more than an inch long. The man alternated at pull, rest, pull, rest, the saw-dust piling up, only strong men making it through a big tree without stopping for a rest. It would be agreed in advance which man would take the saw, and when the tree began to sway, the other man would simply duck out of the way while the man with the saw carried it with him.

Different woods feel different to the saw. Maple is smooth and clean, the dust coming out white and even and smooth, elm tough and dark, the chips more like pieces of sinew.

The rocking motion of the crosscut saw, along with the music of the cutting, makes the work almost a ballet. And to the sound and sight are added the smell of the wood and the way it feels to the sawyer; sometimes we would even taste it, unconsciously seeking to make the experience equally real to all our senses.

So woods were many things to us, tough or yielding, yin and yang.

Sometimes we climbed in the maples, easier trees to reach than the elms, squarer, branches close to the ground even in big trees, as though they kept boys in mind. We carved our initials and our promises in them, knowing always that they were fine trees with solid straight wood that would make into good cabinets or floors or tables, a wood that lasted forever and was always clean, a wood that a boy could look up to.

7. THE SCHOOL

One chilly spring day a year or so ago I walked around on the hill where my elementary school once stood. The building had been gone for a dozen years, hammered down and replaced with a tacky-modern, brick-and-glass-and-plastic, one-story structure across the road where Mark Bott's Jerseys used to loll away the summer afternoons. All the brick and boards and mortar of the two-and-a-half-story old school are gone, probably to fill up a bit of bog somewhere. But as I stood there on the hill, hunched against the icy wind that swept up from my father's farm 100 rods to the west, the building rose again around me, brick and mortar, tone and tissue, and I became, for a little while, a ghost haunting my own memory.

Porches and halls, blackboards and globes, classrooms and the private rooms where the nuns lived, the little chapel, heavy galvanized pipes of swings and slide sets, sturdy old maples in the yard where we played Red Rover, Red Rover, Let Jane Come Over, shouts of play and shy tones of recitations, inkwells and erasers, the fixed society of nuns and a priest and a hundred or so farm kids, tending toward the grubby, virgin in body and mind.

To be honest about it, the school was a creaking old fire-trap, brick and concrete, splintery wooden floors oiled into smoothness and submission by generations of patient nuns and restless youngsters. The air was stuffy, winter and summer; in winter, because the clanking radiators were barely able to cope with the Michigan cold even when all was well, and there was no nonsense of opening windows to allow any unfair competiton; in summer, because it was well known that the alluring sounds of the out-of-doors were more than a match for even the most intimidating nun with a speller or an arithmetic book.

Everything squeaked—the stairs, and the floors, the doors and the desks and the big old globe that hung on a rope, counterweighted, so it could be pulled down from the ceiling at lesson time.

FROM THE LAND AND BACK

The lighting was bad; white globes, hung from the high ceilings, not always with all the bulbs working; high windows, all on the wrong—east—side.

The equipment was bad; the atmosphere too authoritarian to be encouraging to youngsters. The books were few and most of them were out-dated. The nuns, products of a repressive education and schooled as technicians, were ill prepared by any standards.

It was, in short, easily the best educational institution I ever attended.

Most of the ugliness and discomfort prevailed because no one knew any better, and none of us noticed it at the time. This was long before architects scaled schools to conform to the eyes and size of youngsters. Paint protected, it did not decorate, and colors did not matter. In the upper grades the desks were screwed to the floor on long rails, though the first-and-second-grade room—the "baby room," it was called directly enough—had red chairs and tables for certain activities.

No one knew much about educational philosophy; it is not likely that anyone thought much about it. The nuns thought a lot about God and especially about the Virgin Mary, and the priest had the coal bill to concern him. Surely those leathern old German farmers who built the place and kept it up with contributions from the lean land they worked did not think about educational philosophy. Learning was good by definition. So you built a school, with rooms for the desks. You hired nuns—people you could trust, after all—and put them at the front of the rooms and you told your kids that they would by God learn or wish they had. We did.

We memorized. Multiplication tables, all the words in the old green spellers, the songs in the song books, the stories in the Bible history, the questions and answers in the old Baltimore No. 1 catechism: "Q. Why did God make me? A. God made me to know Him, to love Him, to serve Him in this world, and to be happy with Him in the next."

We learned to diagram sentences, and to get the hell out of the building in under three minutes in case anyone ever dropped a forbidden match on one of those tinder-dry, oil-saturated floors, because the whole shebang would have gone up like a Roman candle.

The social power structure was formal, fairly elaborate, rigid, enduring, and could have been studied as though we were Samoan Islanders, for without a doubt to the outsider everything would have been quite transparent.

Officially the nuns held the power, under the benign guidance of the parish priest, who treated them like little children. He was the first benevolent despot in my life. The nuns had the symbols of power. They could scold or praise, punish or reward, pass or fail, or give free time to the well-behaved so that we could nip over to the church to pray for indulgences or sneak up into the choir loft for gamier fun.

But, in fact, much of the power lay in the hands of the older boys, who could exert a day-to-day terrorism over the rest of the school populace. And, more immediately, they could provide a half-day off once or twice each winter, and they did.

Their opportunity came through the coal furnace, a fiery monster of biblical proportions, hidden away in the basement. A select group of seventh- or eighth-graders—of whom I was one, when I reached that eminence—were designated "furnace boys," and among their duties was the responsibility to stoke the heater with coal at frequent intervals. This made it possible for them to leave the room almost at will, without holding up either one or two fingers. They would slip down to the furnace room and shovel lumps of coal into the inferno. Properly fed, the thing would hold a bed of red-white coals a foot deep and two or three feet in diameter, blue flames dancing a painful ballet. As the coals burned out, the boys dug them away. The residue was called clinkers, because when they were hauled out to the dump in a wheelbarrow and dropped, they would clink against the concrete.

Furnace boys had the high privilege of eating their lunch in the furnace room. Seated on sooted benches they would play cards on a broken table, dealing from greasy old decks, gnawing away at thick sandwiches of homemade bread and butter, often with nothing else between the slices.

At some point each winter, on a day when the sledding was especially good and the wind not too cold and the lessons exceptionally tiresome, one or two of the furnace boys would slip down to the furnace room early in the afternoon session. Preparations were carefully made; they would drink water all morning until they practically sloshed when they walked. So primed, they would throw open the door to the firepit and urinate wildly over the glowing coals. The result was an incredibly acrid stench that wafted quickly through the entire school and rendered the building uninhabitable. A recess of at least an hour was mandatory. If we could coax the nuns into joining us on the sleighs and toboggans, we might get them to forget their stern duties and we would be free for an afternoon. The furnace boys always explained solemnly to the nuns that the old furnace had "blown back" again and descend to the basement to make repairs. The rest of the school would pile out of the building and the furnace boys would break out the cards to play pinochle until the stench cleared. If the nuns knew what really caused the smell, they never said. I wonder how they could have asked.

There were three nuns in three classrooms. The "baby room" accommodated grades one and two; the middle room, grades three, four, and five; and the big room, grades six, seven, and eight. Back of the baby room was a little chapel, and sometimes during holy seasons we would attend a service there, the double doors at the back of the room thrown open, and all the school crowding in.

The nuns lived in partially cloistered quarters behind the main stairway, where it was rumored that the sister superior drank a beer on Saturday nights. They were Sisters of Mercy in name and, for the most part, in spirit. Their habits were black, with white fronts starched flat so that the only evidence that they might have had breasts was the odd way that some of the fronts stuck out. Sometimes their affection for one child or another would overwhelm them, and we would be hugged against those crackling paste-boards that smelled of starch like the host we got at the communion rail in church, and we would be terrified that the things would break and we would be in actual contact with those holy bodies. Few of us welcomed such displays of affection. But we all wondered whether they shaved their hair beneath their headdresses. A few who had happened to be in school on weekends claimed that Sister Mary So-and-So had long, flowing, lovely blonde hair. Perhaps.

Some of the nuns were loved, some respected, some feared and hated. When they talked to us about fearing God, things got mixed up a little. We feared Sister Mary So-and-So, we knew, and if fear of God was the same thing, what was so good about that? On the other hand, when another sister talked to us about how much God loved us, her eyes would fill and sometimes she could hardly go on. That we understood. We returned her love, and it was better than fear.

Once when I was in the sixth grade—I know it was the sixth, because I recall where I sat, and it was the section for sixth-graders—we had a nun who was especially nasty. It was one thing to humiliate the slow learner, but another to be constantly sarcastic about it. We all hated her; it was a special kind of hatred, because in that life there were few people to hate. We knew nothing of political figures, so we could not hate them. Some of our fathers, black Republicans all, hated Roosevelt, but by that time we were in war and one does not too actively hate the president when the nation is at war. At least not then and there. There were no evil men in the community to hate; we had no racial contact so there was no outlet for hate there; and when you are twelve or so, it is pretty hard to work up much of a hate for the devil, because you still believe in your own automatic salvation, just as you still believe in your own immortality.

So for many of us this troubled nun was our first experience with hate, and we made the most of it. We talked at length at recess and at noon hour of the horrid things we would like to see happen to her. We planned protests, and how we would write anonymous letters to the priest. Of course this was all talk; had our parents known we had any hint of disrespect for any religious figure, we would have been thrashed beyond reason.

Yet the hate was there, and I, as a show-off, got in trouble because of it. I was a show-off because I was not good at any athletics, or much else out-of-doors, and needed something to show my peers that I deserved their friendship. They did not especially care that I could spell or write verse, so I had to do something. The nun and I had some exchange one afternoon, my side was largely comprised of polite "Yes, s'ter," and "No, s'ter." But as she turned away, I stuck out my tongue. My timing was a fraction off; she saw me out of the corner of her eye and flew into a rage. Screaming at me, she made me come to the front of the room and kneel there, facing the rest of the youngsters, and say, several times, "I'm sorry, class, for what I did."

I can still hear the horrified silence into which I spoke. It still hung over the place as I walked there that cold spring

day not long ago, haunting me with the lesson that this is
not a way to become popular, unless you wish always to
be an outlaw. My friends never spoke of the incident. Had
I gotten away with it, I might have been a bit of a hero.
But I was caught and punished, and perhaps it speaks of
the awe in which we held authority, all authority, that this
tainted me for a time, because however outrageous they all
may have thought my punishment, they showed the syn-
drome that was later found in the inmates of Hitler's death
camps—authority was punishing, so there must have
been a wrong, the punishment must be just.

The other day, I snapped at my youngest son for something. He bridled, telling me in his loudest five-year-old
voice that I was wrong and that I should not yell at him
when he had done something good, not bad. He was completely right; in a moment of irritation with something
else, I had been unfair, and I apologized. I wonder if the
change is the result of environment, the attitude of his parents, or just what. I do know that I never spoke back to a
nun again, and it was not until graduate school that I
found myself able to argue with a professor.

School was a physical frustration to me and, for the
most part, an intellectual lark. Both reactions stemmed
from the same cause. Because of my illness, I had been confined to bed for more than a year just at the preschool age,
and my mother, despairing of entertaining me, had taught
me to read. I am afraid that today I would have had a television set and perhaps never learned to read at all. But as it
was, I was reading perhaps at third-grade level when I entered school. The gap widened, so that by the time I

reached high school, I had consumed probably every book in the township. This made everything else easy, except arithmetic, which I mastered poorly and with great difficulty. But on the other hand I was wearing a brace when I began school; straps of steel, covered with soft leather, that wrapped around me, with little crutches under my arms so that my back would grow straight. It stuck down, and the back of it fitted nicely into the crack at the back of the desk seat, but I still limped rather badly and was not much good at Red Rover, Fox and Geese, or baseball. As time went on, I learned to shoot a fair marble, became the best mumblety-peg player in the school, could ride my bicycle without hands for almost any distance, and stored up enough plenary indulgences on holy days to last me all my natural life.

Whatever else I was, I was not timid, and I was able to join another boy in one fairly profitable protection racket. The object was a fat youngster, a second cousin of mine, in fact, who was especially privileged by his family because his father had wandered away. Not only did his mother pack him a marvelous lunch each day, but he always had money in his pocket so that, if he chose, he could eat in the cafeteria. This cost 10 cents, but he had the cash. So my friend and I, in exchange for not beating the little fellow up, got his lunch each day for most of one long spring. We would hurry down to the cafeteria, gobble down the lunch served there, and find Dennis, trembling, waiting with his big box lunch. Cliff and I would grab it from him, giving a snarl or two, run down to the parish cemetery at the edge of the schoolyard, and, secure in the privacy behind a large tombstone, enjoy a sandwich each, share some fruit. Often, there were two pieces of cake. Poor Dennis was no worse off; a fat boy anyway, he never showed any effects of hunger.

But one day a little boy from town got wind of our racket and told on us. In later years, I have always felt great sympathy for the natural tattletale, the youth so desperate for the approval of authorities that he will rat on his peers, not for any deep-felt reason, but just for the thrill of being briefly on the side of the law. In that period in Germany this youngster might have been a leader among the Hitler Youth. But then, I might have been writing songs for them. In any case, he told, and we were punished a little by nuns who had no real training in how to discipline racketeers, and we had to live on the peanut-butter sandwiches and thin soup and tuna-noodle casseroles that were the standard fare in the cafeteria.

One clung to little privileges. There was a flagpole, and it was a major perquisite to be allowed to run the flag up early in the day and take it down before the bus came. There was no patriotism in this, just ritual, for which we were well conditioned by the church. As I grew stronger, I tried to see how high I could climb on the pole, and made it up two of the three sections, as I recall.

Another perquisite was dusting the blackboard erasers. The felt would clog up with chalk dust, and the way to clean the erasers was to take them out and pound them against the porch or the side of the schoolhouse until the dust was out.

Once in a while, we could fool the nuns into thinking

that we had a fresh devotion and prevail on them to let us slip over to the church to pray. They didn't fall for that very often, though.

There were lines for everything: to go to the cafeteria, to come in from recess, to go to mass, to take the bus. I despise lines these days, and my children miss rides and carnivals sometimes because I will not stand in them. There may be a connection.

One of my happiest years was the fifth grade. The two rows of desks along the east side of the big room on the second floor, the "middle room," where occupied by fifth-graders. I was out of my brace, had some standing with my fellows, and had managed to get a seat near a window. On spring afternoons, I could levitate myself out that window to all the mysteries I knew.

Below, just across the road, was the Bott place, where two bachelor brothers kept a tidy Jersey farm. They had all John Deere equipment, and we watched them at work in all the seasons school kept. We watched their cows wander back across the fields, graze along the creek; we watched the snow fall across the fields in winter and knew that they would green again in the spring. The nuns would have had us believe that this was happening because God willed it so. Somehow, that never stuck. It happened because it was natural for it to happen, and for most of us God in nature was not important. I wonder that more of us did not become scientists. On the other hand, we worried much about God and His threat to our souls. We were much more vulnerable there. Yet none of us became priests either.

FROM THE LAND AND BACK

Beyond the Bott farm the land stretched off to the town, and on fall and spring days when windows were open, we could hear the noon whistle from the grain elevator.

As we grew older, we could see farming going on. Silos were filled before our eyes, and we yearned to be there helping. Grain was planted in the spring before school recessed for the summer. Those windows were our television sets, and they looked out not on a world of fantasy, or animated cartoons and dreamed-up comedy sketches, but on the world that we looked forward to joining. Our imaginations were rooted there in what we saw, and we wanted to be part of it, to grow up naturally to share the scene that other youngsters would look down on from those windows. It was such a logical evolution, such a natural step. Perhaps that was what made the community so stable for all those years, and what made the break so severe when it became impossible for us to be part of that pastoral picture we had looked down at as children.

We learned about God as part of school, or perhaps it is more accurate to say we learned about the church. We memorized things so we could take our first communion while in the first grade. For that occasion the girls were all in white, veils and dresses and stockings and shoes, and new white rosaries, their new prayer books, white too, clasped between their hands. Vestal virgins for Jesus; though there was no cynicism in it for them or for anyone, perhaps not even any knowledge of how the rite hinted of pagan ceremonies.

A few years later came Confirmation, in which we became soldiers of Christ. More lines, marching down the aisles, candles and incense, chants and hymns. The lure of the rituals was so strong that many dreamed of being priests or nuns, taking holy orders, a final decision, a suicide of sorts, an ultimate commitment like that of the man who went over the top to capture a Jap pillbox in the comic books we were reading at the time. A pillbox for Jesus, a flamethrower for the Lord.

Some of us were altar boys. On Saturdays, up before chores, a hurried mass, home to work in the fields. Size 10 cassock, size 16 surplice. Learn to light the incense, swing the censer, carry the candles, which ones to light for different masses, how to snuff them out without smashing them. You were always excused from school if you served mass, or took communion. Then, because we still fasted 12 hours before communion in those days, you had an egg sandwich at your desk, packaged hot in wax paper that morning and, if you were lucky, with the melted butter still warm in the thick homemade bread.

The church was an architectural place for us, bigger even than the barns, and different, haunted by God and the mysterious things that made it special. A friend and I used to make a practice of slipping into the church at noon hour and head for the belfry. In the front doors, quietly up into the choir if no one was around to say no. A stair up at a back corner of the choir loft; a wooden cover at the top of it, to be lifted up and slid aside. Just rafters then; don't step between them. Across to another ladder, up to the base of the belfry. A final short ladder, another covered hole, and we were beside the big bells themselves. All the places to sit were covered with bird dung, but we carried shingles or paper bags to sit on, and peered out through the louvers, with no desire ever to go beyond what we could see.

Panoramic view of the countryside. My father's whole farm below us on one side, with the view continuing to other farms, almost all the way to Mecosta. Remus nearly in sight, in the other direction, but hidden in trees. Far off, 8 or 10 miles away, farms that we would not visit until we had moved on to the consolidated high school and began to date girls who lived on them.

The trip became almost a ritual for us; we could do it even after the first bell rang, 15 minutes before the end of noon hour, and still get back in time.

We mastered the lessons the nuns set for us, gathered eight final report cards, old-fashioned yellow ones with letter grades in every subject every marking period, a complete record, including any disciplinary actions taken against us. The priest came over at the end of the marking periods to hand out the cards. He would examine each one, handing out faint praise for the good grades, gentle criticism for the weak ones.

At the public high school, we joined a group of youngsters less religious, for the most part at least. The town kids seemed more sophisticated, and the ones from other farms seemed more prosperous. We were absorbed in the new experience of a school five times as big as the Catholic elementary school—there were thirty-eight in my senior high school class, more than one-third the number in the entire eight grades at the Catholic school. And we were

going through the agonies of adolescence and finding ourselves, and I doubt that anything the least bit extraordinary
happened in high school.

We came back to the Catholic school to attend the
meetings of the youth group, meetings planned to keep us
from drifting away from our faith. Otherwise we grew
away from the school so quickly that we never went back
to visit, as we did on occasion to the high school.

As I stood there that day in the cold, haunting and remembering, I realized that I was not the only ghost
around.

Here was "Smokey," a bag of nerves and key center
fielder, who always had trouble getting his bowels to move
quickly enough so that he would not miss the first inning
or two of the game.

And my two friends named Mike, who may never have
been closer than the day one hit the other and broke a
bone in his hand.

And Keith, whom I used to threaten for some forgotten
reason, and who is now at least twice as big as I. And
Mary Margaret and Bonnie, a year older, wealthy girls,
unattainable, clean hair and barrettes, grown up, distant,
early objects of my imagined lust, not noticing me.

And a big boy my age, who fell steadily behind year by
year because he was not quite right, friendly, stupid, always smelling a little of urine—his own, not that of the
cows.

And the family we always thought of as being poor, because when times were worst they carried lard sandwiches for their lunch, and we never got poorer than bean sandwiches.

All ghosts with me there in the schoolyard, all gone away now, perhaps having forgotten all this, though of course it is still a part of them. The warmth of remembering went out of me, and I was left cold and alone again. The wind chilled, and I hurried to the warm car and drove away.

8. THE TOWN

Our town was an honest little place, with no pretensions and no right to any. It had no glamour and laid claim to none. It had no beauty and no chamber of commerce to pretend that it did. It never promised, so it never disappointed. It was simple and direct, built to serve a limited purpose, serving that and no more, never confusing itself. Yet it was to me what New York is to a native. It wasn't much of a town, but we didn't know that, and it was all the town we had.

FROM THE LAND AND BACK

When I was preparing for a career in journalism, a wise old professor gave me good advice. Begin your career in a small town, he told me. The same things happen there that happen in a big town, but they are easier to find out about. It didn't occur to me at the time, but that was true of Remus, too. All the things that happen in a city happened there, and they were all embodied in individuals—The Barber, The Mechanic, The Grocer, The Banker, The Hardware Man, The Doctor—generally one in each category, all free to develop in my mind and in reality as characters, and develop they did. I have never been certain whether they live in my memory as characters because they had more foibles and eccentric traits than people anywhere else, or simply because we knew them so well over such a long period of time and observed them at such leisure. There is little anonymity in a small town.

The town is called Remus not because of any association with mythology, but because the first white child born in the area was given that name. We used to talk about this —"the first white child"—with the same simple prejudice that people use when they talk about the settling of the West—"the first white men in the area." There were black families in Remus, both townsmen and farmers, and we really did not know that some of them had not been there first. But the habit persisted—"the first white child." There was an Indian reservation only a few miles away, but none of us gave that any thought at all.

The town was first called Wheatland Center, a designation with a pretentious ring that collapsed under the impact of reality. Wheatland is the name of the township and

THE TOWN

Remus is in its precise center, but I imagine that it was either a promoter or a dreamer who thought the area would be a rich wheat land. It didn't take long for people to see that it never would.

During my father's youth there were dirt streets and board sidewalks; in the depression a public works project replaced them with concrete paving. Small towns in those days got a mile of pavement, and when you reached the end of the pavement, you were dumped without ceremony back onto the dirt and gravel of the local road. We would ride our bikes the two miles to town just for the fun of speeding around on the pavement.

Change has been incredibly lacking. No big buildings have burned or been built in my lifetime; no more than a dozen new houses have gone up, and those all in the last decade. The town remains almost exactly as it was thirty-five years ago.

The farms that the town grew up to serve have changed—fewer cattle, larger holdings, some unused land, less activity for the most part. The town will probably have to change before long. Perhaps someone will build a factory there, and the economy will pick up and the air will go sour. In the meantime, though, it remains a social and economic backwater, strangely untouched, and all the characters are remembered. Some of them are still around.

The hardware store was an institution, and the man who ran it little less so. It was the biggest hardware store I have ever seen, and this is not a boy's selective memory. The place must have been built as a hay barn, for there are soaring lofts and back rooms and warehouses filled with incredible inventories of obsolete junk.

The owner was a silent man. When you needed something, you walked into his store and he waited patiently behind the counter for you to tell him why you were there. People did not go there to shop; they went because they needed a plow point or a harness part or a gear for a binder. Whatever it was, he had it, his mind a filing case for the endless bins and drawers where uncounted odds and ends of machinery waited to be needed.

It was said that he could still build a Model T Ford from spare parts as late as 1950. This may not have been true, but it could have been. One day I was cutting hay with a neighbor, towing a mower that had been designed for horses and converted so we could pull it with the tractor. The machine had been obsolete for twenty years and had not been a popular model when it was in production. We hit a rock and broke the pitman rod—a wooden stick that converts the rotary motion of the gear wheels to the back-and-forth motion of the sickle bar. This was as it should be; the pitman was designed to break, protecting the rest of the machine from damage. But the advanced age of the equipment probably meant we would have to make a new one by hand. First, though, let's check with the Hardware Man. He inspected the broken part, searching for the number, tilting his head far back. Then he went away, back into one of the rooms where those bins were piled to a two-story ceiling, and he wrestled a ladder into place, climbed up, and came down with the part. He looked at the price—probably fixed when he stocked it twenty years earlier—and told us how much, and we paid and went back to work.

After the war, another hardware store opened. My father went in one day to buy something, and the man charged more than was marked on the item, explaining that prices had gone up since it had been stocked. My father exclaimed in some outrage that the store operator had not paid the new higher price and so should not charge it. The owner replied that my father didn't understand modern business practices. I suppose he was right.

The Mechanic was an oddly muddled man for that town. He had odds and ends of talent that barely made a whole, but he bunched them together in a kind of makeshift fashion to profess a skill and make a living. He probably knew more about the insides of the old flat-head Ford V-8 than anyone outside the Ford engineering department. It was a skill that endured fairly well; the same engine was used in Fords, almost unchanged, for nearly a quarter of a century. First there were the depression years, when old machinery had to be kept going because no one could afford new. Then came the war years, when old machinery had to be kept going because new things were not being made. Those were good times to be a mechanic.

He was also a musician. He and his wife made up a pitiful little band, she with a good strong piano, he with drums and cymbals. They were booked by high schools for dances on weekends, but they never learned the new music that came home from the war, and their instruments gathered first dust, then rust.

He drove a school bus, too. Morning and night, every

school day, he swung the big Dodge bus out across the countryside, picking up a load of kids on a 20- or 30-mile route, taking them home again at 4 o'clock. On the last day of school, before a holiday, he would run the home trip backwards sometimes, putting the last-gathered children off last, giving them a chance to see a little of the countryside. And when the youngsters who rode his bus —I rode with him for twelve years—finished high school, he gave us each a little verse that he had written himself, an individual verse for each one.

And he drank—perhaps never drunk, but little quick trips up the street to the bar for a glass of wine. There were rumors and shielded dark conversations about that; did he drive the school bus while drunk? The youngsters defended him to a man, and the question was never pressed.

He and his wife lived in a little apartment over the garage, smells of oil and grease floating up to them. He could fix bikes, too, or at least he would try. He gave up the garage a few years ago, and I do not know whether it was because he was old or because he no longer understood the cars. His son works in another garage, is a good mechanic. I might ask him, but I don't think I could.

The Barber looked like a dean. A tall man, spectacled, white-haired, thin, he walked with a measured tread, wore a necktie. He enjoyed enduring local fame because he once killed a bear while hunting. His little shop was quiet most of the week, and as you walked by, he might be dozing in the chair or reading an American Legion magazine. I think he fought in World War I, and, like all men who one time in their lives take part in something too big for them to understand, he was forever changed. On Saturday the shop was filled with farmers and their sons, in for Saturday night. He stayed open late, clipping steadily, often with a helper, the hair piling up on the floor, no precautions against disease.

Until a short time ago, there was probably less change in barbers' shops than anywhere else. Then suddenly, as such changes come these days, hair went long again, women began coming into men's shops, prices went even higher, and long lists of services began to appear. My barber today is constantly badgering me about the chemical balance of my scalp. On occasion, it has occurred to me that the Remus barber, like the mechanic, got out just in time.

The Banker was an awesome, distant figure. He was a last resort for loans, for money borrowed against the land itself, a desperate measure taken only in the most extreme circumstances once the mortgage was off the land.

Casual attitudes about home ownership are common these days. People refinance to put their children through college or to take a trip, and they trade up in houses as they trade up in cars. For a long time, I thought people kept their property neat and painted and improved because they wanted to express pride of ownership. But for most, it is either a restlessness or a continuing hedge against the day when the house will be sold as they move on. None of this was true then. A man's place was his place, as long as he lived. And once that first crushing mortgage was lifted, title to the land was to be kept clear at any price. Keep the banker away, stay out of debt. It was a man guarding his cave, a mother her nest.

Wealthier families had checking accounts, I suppose, or otherwise had money in the bank. The first time I ever saw a personal check, written by one man to another, was when I was in college. I was working on a Saturday for a professor, putting up storm windows. He wrote me a check for my day's work, and I was amazed that a man who worked only with his mind could be so wealthy.

The bank was tiny, and I don't think anyone ever tried to rob it. One glance would have been enough to turn a robber away. In the early 1950s my mother used to check the annual reports, predicting with confidence that the assets would soon grow to a million dollars. We had no idea it could grow so big.

The Banker must have been a lonely man, for if there was anyone in that town who could hail him over for a game of cards and a beer, I can't imagine who it could have been. He lived in a big old house about two blocks from the bank—nearly at the edge of town—and had little to do with our lives. Yet it was one of my father's proudest boasts that he could always go in and borrow money if he needed it, because his name was good. He urged us to keep the name good, so we could borrow money too. That was the way banks were in those days.

The Doctor was a parody of a Norman Rockwell painting. A small, round man, he seemed to me to have been born with white hair. And with a vest on. His rounds were from house to house, not from bed to bed in a hospital. I remember him driving awkwardly around in an old Plymouth coupe, the kind with only one seat and no rumble. Children were born at home in those days, and if we got sick we went to his office and waited our turn. In the records my father kept for 1935, I find no indication that any money changed hands over my birth.

Medical care was one of the worst parts of life in that town and in that time; it began only in recent years. Look at any old cemetery and see the appalling number of infant graves, and remember that most were left unmarked. Doctors knew so little, had so little to work with. It is no wonder that we remember them with such fondness . . . the ones who had cause to doubt their ability are not around to remember.

The Grocer was altogether out of place, a man born too soon. He was always hustling, dealing, giving the appearance of trying to expand his store, build up business. I always thought that the town owed him a lot more than it ever realized. As much as anyone, he brought a touch of progress, a hint of the future. He eventually built a small chain of little stores, but his efforts at getting rich were doomed. There was simply too little money in the community, no way to pull it together in a pile big enough to make anyone rich.

Remus was first and last a working town, a farmer's town. The grain elevator blew the noon whistle. If you wanted to buy clothing you chose from anything on the rack in the dry-goods store, and if what you needed wasn't in the hardware store or the dime store, a trip to the county seat was in order.

Yet the town was more than enough for a boy seeing it occasionally from the farm. There were alleys, forming spaces not like anything on the farm. And there were strange boys, who might be bullies and from whom you would run. There were girls to whisper about, good towels in the bathrooms, and a blinker light where the two highways met and where you could sit and watch for new cars.

There was another town, Mecosta, two miles in the other direction, an odd little place left over from the logging days, getting a bit of resort business in the summer from people who stayed at the lakes nearby. There is no particular reason for Mecosta to survive, though it has acquired the writer Russell Kirk as a resident and he has written about its odd ghostly quality. The single street is so wide it makes the town seem abandoned much of the time; stores change hands, businesses come and go, and there seem to be no roots going out from it. When we were boys, we used to call it "Brigadoon" and drive over now and then to see if it was still there. Even after I drive through it now, I am never quite sure. But its bank was robbed by a trusted employee, there have been fights in its bars, and the main store, where we traded when I was small, burned. It is a town that seems always on the verge of fading away, yet on its good days it is more lively than Remus. Strange winds blow there, and odd sounds are heard in the night. Perhaps the ghosts of the lumbermen are keeping it alive, knowing they will need it later.

Trains don't stop in Remus any more, save now and then to drop off a car of feed and pick up a carload of grain from the elevator. Remus can be served over the road, and the arrival of the beer truck from Mount Pleasant is more of an event than the train ever was.

Now and then, I have thoughts of some day starting a weekly paper there, and living quietly. But I don't think enough happens to fill even a little news space. I don't know what I would write about. There is no need for the stores to advertise much, and the population has not gone up from the 600 it was forty years ago. I don't know who would read the paper, outside of the ministers, and there are only two or three of them.

But the town has never said, come, this would be a good place to publish a little weekly paper. It keeps its honesty, the petty purity that comes so easily to men and towns when the stakes are low.

9. MECHANIZATION

It is probably not coincidence that the process of mechanizing American farms seems to resemble the process of mechanizing wars. In the beginning, men walked around with sharp sticks of one kind or another in their hands. Soldiers poked them at each other; farmers poked around in the dirt with them. We developed axes of various sorts, to fell trees or members of the opposing army. Crude instruments followed; there is a startling similarity between the catapults used for chucking rocks at castles and the devices that pulled stumps from land we wanted to put to crops. Early tractors clanked around awkwardly like the first tanks; by the time the Panzers and Shermans were running smoothly with automatic transmissions and V-8 engines, tractors had rubber tires, high-speed road gears, and self-starters.

And now, when soldiers commute to battle by helicopter and airplanes are used for any number of ghoulish tasks, farmers sit in self-propelled harvesters with air-conditioned cabs, checking computers for dairy cattle rations, and the cows are milked in sanitary places called parlors, often built with glassed fronts if the barn is near a highway, presumably so tourists can watch.

The chemistry of war is a little ahead, I think—smokeless powder and rockets preceded DDT and other insecticides.

This is not coincidental, because both areas of human endeavor are involved with struggle—war against people presumed to be enemies, though it rarely turns out that way in the long run, and agriculture in combat with the environment. There the danger is that we might conquer so completely that the environment will cease to fight back; it may just lie down and die, and then of course we will too. International wars became implicitly impossible when the atomic bomb was perfected. The only result of an atomic war is defeat for the species and probably the planet. But the chemistry of agriculture is only a little behind; some of the advanced poisons may make that part of the battle impossible one day, too. Once in a while, it seems only a matter of time.

FROM THE LAND AND BACK

Like the social revolution that came inevitably to the farm when isolation ended, the technological revolution was so sudden and so complete that no one had time to consider what parts of it were good and which needed a little more thought. We bought hay choppers in the first place for the same reasons we go to the moon; we found out we could, and so we thought we must.

It all began so innocently. There have been tools for millions of years. and always an inexorable pressure to make them better, more efficient, more powerful. The effort made a quantum leap in my father's lifetime.

My grandfather homesteaded with oxen and horses. Their muscle and his own were the machines that did the work. The energy to fuel the machines was all grown on the land, all taken from the soil he owned. He pulled the stumps with horses and a clumsy device hung from poles arranged above the stump. A series of pulleys multiplied the power of a team of horses until they could lift the stump out of the ground. The softer the soil, the easier the stumps came loose, which was a further incentive to pull the pine stumps from the sandy soil, rather than tackling the problems of hardwood trees on heavy soil.

For a long time, planting was done by hand. In many of the sheds and barns of that country, there are little one-man corn planters still hanging on the walls, left there when last used, and forgotten. The planter has a round hopper on the front of a thin board, with a grip at the top like the end of a shovel handle. The bottom has a steel point. This is thrust into the earth, then the device is bent forward. A pedal sticks out in front and trips the disk at the bottom of the hopper to release the corn which falls down into the soil. The man steps on the corn hill as he moves on, packing the soil around the seed. This sounds like a slow process, and it is, but a man can plant a couple of acres a day and if he is relying on a team for power to plow, till, cultivate, and harvest, two or three days of planting will put in all the corn he can care for. The rows were marked by chains hung from a pole. Two men, or a man and his wife, would carry the pole along, allowing the chains to drag so they would mark the soil. If you carried the chains both ways on a field, you had a crisscross pattern. The corn hills would be planted where the lines crossed. The result was a field with rows in both directions. Later on, the same thing was accomplished with planters which would "checkrow." This need for cross-cultivation was eliminated when tractors were used to cultivate, for they could travel faster and throw the earth up higher around the corn plant, covering weeds. Still later, insecticides came into wider use as weed killers and some corn growers now cultivate hardly at all.

Use of such primitive devices passed beyond skill and became an art. Some men developed such a measured pace with the hand corn planter that they could cultivate both ways without the additional trip with the markers. They took as much pride in their careful planting as their sons took in learning to plow or plant straight furrows and rows with tractors.

Grain was still sown with a hand seeder in my father's youth. You walked along at a steady pace, holding a cloth basket of grain with a spreading device at the bottom. The spreader was spun with a crank at the side, and only the most skillful men could manage even coverage. It was not a job for a windy day. A team of horses pulled a culti-packer over the field to cover the seed and tuck the soil around it. Grain drills, much more precise, followed. They made it possible to fertilize at the same time, and to sow grass seed as well.

My grandfather harvested some of his grain with a scythe and cradle. Again, it was a skilled task, making the great swoop with the long scythe, sliding the grain off carefully from the cradle, and laying it in a little pile. A man's wife or children followed, tying the grain into bundles, using little ropes of grain stalks for twine. These people had an easy communion with Ruth and Boaz.

The bundles were piled into shocks to be hauled to the barn for threshing when they were dry. This meant handling the grain three times in the field, twice in the barn. The combine, which does the work in a single trip through the field, was a genuine advance. It is difficult for me to realize that the combine first came to that area in my youth, and as I grew up, many farmers still did not trust it and continued to use the thresher.

The threshing machine was the Trojan horse that brought the internal combustion engine to the farm, and it was a development that could not be held back. Early threshers were powered by steam engines; the power was still generated by the land, as stumps and straw made the heat for the steam. But then threshing machine engines had to have kerosene or gasoline. The farmer became dependent on a supplier for his power.

Out on the plains, where there were acres to turn around on, the tractors had been moving in from the turn of the century. But in fields of 5 or 10 acres, the big tractors were too clumsy. International Harvester and Ford made the breakthroughs, the former largely by mistake. They had developed an F-12 model—F for Farmall and 12 for the horsepower rating—for cultivating cotton in the South, and somehow a few of them slipped north. They caught on quickly, and a slightly more powerful F-14 followed, then the classic F-20, with its raised axles to clear row crops.

The F-12 was a harsh, uncompromising machine, all iron and steel and square corners, rather like a tractor a child would make up from a big Erector set. Everything was iron, from the single tire in front to the high wheels and the platform at the rear. At first, these machines were for cultivating only and had no drawbar to which trailing implements could be hitched; farmers welded these on, but they were far from standard. They had three forward speeds, with a maximum speed of perhaps 5 miles an hour. The shifting lever was a stick of iron that wore smooth and paintless over the years, but never softened. The steering wheel was iron. The seat was of steel, though it had a spring. All the parts were sticks or straps of steel, cut or bent or beaten into shape. Rounded gas tanks and radiators were the only hint of streamlining.

Later, the steel wheels were replaced with big rubber tires. A "step-up" transmission became available, which provided a higher range of speeds by multiplying the gears much as an overdrive, or the second axle in some trucks.

FROM THE LAND AND BACK

What the F-12 could do was turn around. There were puny little individual brakes, close in on the transmission, that could be worked by hand. A plate affixed to the front wheel turned like a Cyclops's eye and was connected to the brakes when the cultivator was attached. When you turned the steering wheel all the way in either direction, these rods would set the brake on the inside wheel and the little tractor would turn directly around, the inside wheel serving as a pivot. This was as good as any team could do, and the corn rows could go right to the fence, needing only 10 or 12 feet for the turning.

Ford, with an eye toward helping the small farmer and making a profit at the same time, brought out a small tractor shortly after World War I. It was powered by about the same motor as the Model T and was much more clumsy than the little Farmall. Yet many of them were sold, and now and then you can see one on a junk yard, or in a museum; for years I have not seen one that ran, though the old Farmalls still pop up now and then.

Those noisy old Fordsons had mounted plows, the ancestors of the modern three-point-hitch equipment that is standard on most small tractors. The plow was raised and lowered by hand, hydraulics not yet having been perfected for that purpose, and most farmers thought they would simply not work. Of course they were a hint of the future.

A neighbor owned one of the first Fordsons. He farmed an 80 that lies above my father's farm where we could always look up and see him at work, and he could look down to see us. As the years drew on and the Fordson aged, it developed a deep growl in its gears that could be heard all across our farm. The image of the old man jolting along on his Fordson, standing because no man could last long sitting on that wretched seat, singing at the top of his lungs, and the groan from the tractor's innards drifting down across our farm, is one of the pictures I shall carry in my mind for all time. It was, after all, opera of a sort.

Our second tractor was much more modern. An Oliver 60, we bought it new just before World War II and were lucky to have a dependable tractor in those years when all the factories were turning out other kinds of things. I spent much of my early teens on that 60. It was stylish by comparison with the earlier machines; green and yellow, decorative grill and sexy little mini-fenders, gearshift knob and steering wheel of hard rubber, a self-starter, gauges and a throttle mounted on the steering column, handy to the fingertips.

The four-cylinder engine developed some 18 horsepower at the drawbar, the brakes were better, and the muffler made it quieter. That tractor filled the place in my youth that a Corvette may fill in the life of a rich man's son. But it was more, for it was part of the mission we all shared, and it came to live with us like a member of the family. It had four forward speeds, which moved the tractor at 2½, 3½, 4½, and 6 miles an hour. Second and third were major field gears; fourth for light work and going to and from the field; first was used only for an emergency. Generally, the tractor would spin its wheels in second if the load would not move, so first was of little use.

The Oliver tilled our fields, cultivated the crops, harvested them, powered the silo filler and the combine, hauled wagons, and taught me to respect machinery. We tore the motor apart every second or third year for an overhaul, and it would be like new again.

After the war, my father bought a faster Ford tractor; then another and another. The Oliver was sold to a neighbor, who patched together parts and farmed with it into the 1970s, as the tractor passed its thirtieth birthday. The last time I saw it working, it was smoking a little, and I think it needs an overhaul again.

In the early years of the century no farmer in our area could afford a thresher for his own use, so cooperatives were formed to buy and operate the big machines. At threshing time, the company would set out a route, and the machine would be taken out of storage—usually the barn of one of the members—and tuned up for the season. There were great grease cups to be cleaned and filled, bearings to be adjusted, screens to scrub, and belts and chains and canvas to tighten. A big tractor was needed to power the thresher; our community had at first an old Hart Parr, then an Oliver 99.

Threshing time was a seasonal social event, an observation of the climax of another year, a time to help and share, and for the younger farmers, a time to inspect their neighbors' barns and livestock and fences and see how things were with them.

The farm wives had their own competition at the dinner table, too. It was unusual to manage more than a couple of hours threshing in the morning, but there was always a break at noon, and the wife of the farmer whose grain was being threshed set the table for all hands. To anyone who has lived through a threshing season, the term "groaning board" makes sense. The tables literally groaned under the weight of the food set on them.

There were potatoes, usually mashed and served in great earthen bowls, to be covered with meat gravy or butter or both. There were casseroles of various kinds, often half a dozen; servings of squash and pumpkin, vegetables from the garden, perhaps roast corn; roast pork or beef, maybe chicken and dumplings as a side dish. There were coffee and milk to drink. Dessert was huge pies and cakes, and you were encouraged to sample two or three kinds.

When this feast was done, the diners would stagger outside, hoping to nap off their gluttony under the trees before resuming work by 1 o'clock. Sedentary men would gain a dozen pounds in the threshing season. But the work was so hard, the hours so long, that only the men who were naturally heavy anyway would put on weight. The rest would sweat the calories away in the fields and the mow and at home in the early mornings and evenings, when they had to keep up their own chores.

Threshing, like haying, was incredibly filthy work. The straw is scratchy and usually long sleeves were in order to protect the forearms. A few of the older men always left their sleeves rolled down in any case and kept their collars buttoned. My own father expressed his independence and progressive attitude by always rolling up the sleeves of his blue work shirts, always leaving them open at the throat. In later years he even abandoned his bib overalls for belted ones, denim slacks, levis, again now in favor among the undergraduates and for the same reason my father liked them; they are incredibly durable and easy to care for.

The dust from the threshing machines rises up in a cloud like the mushroom above an atomic bomb. But the machine was usually inside the barn, and so the cloud settled down over men and machine, coating all with a thick layer of harvest fall-out. It is uncomfortable, but it is not lethal. Most of it washed off at the outside pump at the end of the day.

A boy would work the pump while the men lined up, ducking their heads under the spout, splashing water over face and neck and arms, sluicing away the worst of the dust. To accomplish this in a shower would be almost impossible, because by the time you got to the shower in most modern houses you would have made the rest of the rooms uninhabitable. As you walked, great clouds of dust rose as the dirt shook loose from high shoes and socks, from overalls and shirts, from any hair that stuck out from under the straw hat. Even after the bout with the pump, you had to be swept off with a broom, before you could come inside to tidy up.

The job of threshing was a hot and filthy one, but it was in no way disagreeable. There was a pride in how dirty one got; a mark of honest work, performed in the interests of the harvest. There was a social, indeed ceremonial, aspect to it all; like being bloodied in combat, one wore one's dirt and fatigue with pride, and even the most fastidious mother and housewife would allow a layer of dirt that would bring a stern word at any other occasion.

In the winter, the women at their quilting bees would

hold long conversations about the food they had prepared. The men discussed the dishes enough to encourage competition, but even poor cooking was tolerated, because what the men wanted was great quantities of food. If it was good, that was a bonus, but the job of fueling the body was foremost.

I recall one such occasion when my mother brought in a lemon meringue pie, one of her specialities, and served it with considerable pride. A man sitting at my left forked up a big mouthful, and as he chewed into it, a strange look settled on his features. He put the fork down, swallowed the bite as best he could, and washed it down with water. My mother was puzzled. I had not observed his discomfort and took a big bite too. I was less slow about pointing out the trouble; she had forgotten to add sugar.

The threshing machines were big, heavy, and clumsy. They rolled on comparatively small steel wheels and were sometimes difficult to maneuver into barns. Most barns in that area are bank barns, meaning that they are built into the side of the hills, with the lower floor where the livestock were housed entered on ground level on one side, and the threshing floor, on the opposite side, was also entered at grade. But few hills really have that sharp a grade, and usually the entry to the threshing floor was built up and fairly steep. A team would have little trouble pulling a load of grain or hay up the hill, but backing the thresher in with a tractor was often another matter. My grandfather's barn on the family home place presented such a problem, for besides being steep, the entry was sandy. The small steel wheels of the thresher cut into the sand, multiplying the power needed to push it, and if the tractor began to spin or skid sideways, there was nothing to do but back all the way down the hill and begin again. Pushing the thresher into the barn became one of the skills that was talked about; a man who could do it with some regular success earned much respect from his neighbors.

The custom of sharing work with the thresher was one of the origins of an almost communal aspect of farm life in that area which came to full flower in the first years after World War II. Another was the need to share help in filling silos, which resulted in another company's being formed to buy a silo filler and keep it in repair. The members of the company moved from farm to farm for that job just as they did for threshing.

The silo filler, which simply chopped whole corn and blew it up into the silo, required somewhat less power than the thresher. Farmers took turns running it with their own tractors. Our Oliver 60 could run it, but it was not really powerful enough to take the full capacity of the cutter, and if one was not careful, the stream of chopped green corn spurting up the long pipe to the top of the silo would slow and then suddenly stop going over the top. The result would be plugged pipes. The equipment would be shut down, a plate at the bottom of the pipe removed, and the plug pulled out, handful by handful.

One neighbor had a Farmall H, which was slightly more powerful. But the best power, until the big tractors began to come into the area during the war, was supplied by the John Deere A owned by another neighbor.

In those days John Deeres were simple almost to the

point of being primitive. Other tractor engines had four or six cylinders; the John Deere had two. Other tractors had self-starters or cranks; the John Deere had a big exposed fly wheel which the driver pulled over to start the engine. John Deeres were big and green and had hand clutches; they were easy and cheap to repair, and the putt-putt sound when they worked made them identifiable for miles. We called them "square wheelers" and considered them efficient but less pleasant than other tractors. But when we put Leo's old A into the belt and opened the throttle, the cutter would throw a stream of corn as big as a man's thigh into a 40-foot silo as fast as two men could stuff the corn into the mouth. Leo would lean against the wheel of the tractor, sucking at a broken stub of a pipe, a hint of a smile on his face, while the motor pulled so hard that the front wheels nearly came off the ground under the force of the explosion of the two big pistons.

Later on, Leo and his A were outmoded by younger men and faster tractors. One of my last silo-filling assignments at Dad's farm entailed staying inside the silo with Leo, stamping around and around in the fresh chopped corn all day, packing it down so the subsequent settling would not be so great, taking off the lengths of filler pipe as the level in the silo rose. Late in the day, a neighbor smuggled a pint of whiskey into the silo and I had a pull or two. I was probably seventeen, and this was my first serious taste of whiskey. As we reached the top of the silo, I felt a call of nature and jumped up to a board laid across the open top. Swaying a little, I proceeded to urinate off the 36-foot high perch. Leo began to sputter, and might have fainted in alarm, only I fell backward off the board into the silo, as I finished the task. My father would not have approved.

Another memorable event occurred one year when the corn froze early, and we jammed it into the silo although it was a little unripe for that purpose. This made for excess moisture, and at the bottom, where the pressure was greatest and the fermentation at its peak, the corn turned into a crude and bitter sort of corn whiskey. We discovered this fact one day when the hogs got out and found the juice oozing from the silo. They lapped it up eagerly, and we were faced with a dozen or fifteen drunken hogs, who could hardly keep their feet as we tried to herd them back to the pen amid gales of laughter at their antics. Every time they fell, they would squeal, and a clumsy confused drunken hog is one of life's truly funny sights.

The habit of sharing labor and equipment reached its height in the exuberant years just after the war, when the young men came home, full of plans and impatience, with money in their pockets saved during the long months when there was only fighting and no time to spend any. In many cases mustering-out pay went to buy farms and put in new equipment.

When our neighbor Otto's son acquired the farm from his father by the promise of keeping his parents for the rest of their lives, he built a new concrete silo, bought a new Ford tractor—the first tractor for that farm; the son did not share his father's distrust of equipment—and put plumbing in the house. Others bought milking machines and coolers and began to sell Grade A milk whole for bottling, instead of separating it and selling only the cream. They bought combines and hay balers and field tillers. They took short courses at Michigan State to learn more about farming and rushed home from class to put the new ideas to work the next day. That was a time of much new energy, new ideas, and some new capital, and it marked the beginning of the changes that would end twenty years later with many of the fields abandoned, and among fifty or so farms in the immediate area only one or two actually being the sole support of their proprietors.

But of course we did not know what direction the revolution would take; like political revolutionaries, we simply had the notion that the old order should be changed, that it needed up-dating, and that we were just the ones to do it. The end result would take its own shape, and we would benefit from it. Although the farmers would deny it, much of their thinking was similar to that of Jerry Rubin and Mario Savio. As with most revolutions, the one we worked on the farm was successful, but the goal we gained was not what we wanted, and someone else will have to try again.

I say, "we," including myself in all this, because, although I was only ten when the war ended, I identified with this new wave of work and improvement as the junior high school student today identifies with the campus rebel. I must admit to my part in making the change.

In those first few years we shared everything, with a casualness that dismayed the older men, who had a firmer sense of individual property; our practice would have fascinated a sociologist and delighted a communist. And, for a little while, it worked the way the social theorists like to think it will work; the utopians would have been proud of us.

If a man needed a second wagon for hurrying his haying, he would swing over to a neighbor's and borrow one. If the neighbor was not at home, he would borrow it anyway, and the reciprocity was so easy and automatic that there was never any resentment. A farmer would have a cultivator on his tractor; if another man wanted to cultivate, he might drive his own tractor over to the neighbor's, leave it behind, take the one with the cultivator already mounted, and return it full of gas when the work was done. One farmer would bale another's hay in exchange for having his grain combined. Another would cultivate another man's corn in exchange for the promise of help at silo-filling time. For a time my father had two tractors, and I can recall any number of occasions when we would go to the shed after morning chores and find one tractor, or none, or three; if one was missing, there might be no indication of where it was.

The sharing became so common and so complex that everyone stopped trying to keep track of anything. We all had crops to put out, cattle to care for, and harvesting to do. We took it upon ourselves to make sure that everyone's work got done on time. This applied in cases of illness; if a man was unable to work for a while, the group closed around him, milking his cows and tending his fields.

In my personal memory, the system reached its most complex point when a neighbor had a collie pup that I wanted. He was asking ten dollars, which might as well have been a hundred. But I was a skilled tractor driver, and

MECHANIZATION

I earned the dog by taking one man's tractor, hitching it to a disk owned by another, and working a field owned by a third man, in which the brother of the man who owned the dog planned to plant corn. Somehow the slate was wiped clean, and I had the dog.

Presently, however, the balance was upset by the mechanization that created it. The tractors became bigger, the basic machinery simpler to operate. The need for sharing labor was gone.

Hay balers are a good example. The first ones needed at least half a dozen men. One man drove the tractor; as many as four might ride the baler to tie the wires by hand, divide the bales, and do other chores to help the machine along. The bales were forced up a long chute that stuck out behind the baler, and two men on a wagon that was towed along piled up the bales. In a few years, the balers became dependably automatic. Now one man controls the whole operation from the tractor, and the baler not only ties the knots but tosses the bales up into a wagon. The wagons have high racks, and the bales are not stacked neatly but simply allowed to pile up. When the rack is full, the tractor hauls the wagon to the barn, and the bales are kicked out into another conveyor which dumps them into the mow. Again, they are not stacked; those old barns have so much excess mow room that neatness is not required.

Where a crew of men once traveled around threshing, one man now drives a combine around the field, the grain running into a large hopper on the machine. When the bin is full, the grain is dumped into a wagon or a truck parked in the field. A couple of wagons can handle what a combine can harvest in a day, and the grain can be dumped into granaries overnight. If the farmer wants the straw for bedding for the cattle, it can be picked up by the baler.

More important, though, was the economic value of the work done. Sharing was fine when one man's labor could be fairly equated with another's, or when a wagon and a cultivator and a disk all had about the same value.

But a baler costs more, and it wears out. Combines had to be amortized and paid for, and cash came to dominate the transactions. A few men bought tractors with two or three times the work power of others; the exchange was no longer equal.

Sizes and quantities changed, too. A silo 9 feet across does not hold much more than one 8 feet across, if both are about 30 or 35 feet high, as was standard then. But a neighbor built one 12 feet wide and 40 feet high; it holds nearly twice as many tons as a 10 by 40. Another man might have thirty cows and 40 acres of potatoes; his needs for labor and machines were far beyond those of the man with ten cows and 5 acres of potatoes.

So, although we did not know it at the time, we learned a valuable lesson about communal living. It will work only as long as all the members have approximately equal needs, as long as the technology remains roughly static, and while ambitions do not press men to expand their efforts. I know of no situation in which those conditions persist for any length of time.

I also learned something useful about machinery, equipment, perhaps even technology.

MECHANIZATION

It was soon apparent that in many cases the new combines, or choppers, or field tillers were not being bought on a basis of calculated economics. A man with 20 acres of grain to harvest each year has no need for a combine of his own, when he can hire a man to do the work for him for $125 or so; he cannot justify, on economic grounds, the purchase of a combine costing $1,000 or more. The same rules apply, though the figures are different, to the other machines—balers, choppers, and so on. Yet the farmers bought them, along with big tractors to run them. For years, I thought they were simply bad managers, not aware of, or at least not making use of, simple management techniques.

But I see now how alluring machinery is, simply in its nature. A man wanted his own combine, partly because it might give him a sense of independence, but also because it is a universal ego satisfaction to dominate a complicated machine.

More commonly, we see a factory worker who is unable to afford good clothes, first-rate medical care, or good auxiliary educational tools for his children, and perhaps lives in poor housing as well, but who drives to work in an automobile which cost him half or a third of his annual salary and which he will trade for another, equally expensive, long before it has begun to wear out. He bought it in the first place because it was a dream, a vision of himself, strong and handsome, serene in his domination of this machine. Of course it betrays. After the first flush of ownership has worn away, he must admit to himself that the new car gets him to the factory or office no quicker than the one he has traded. But he cannot admit his mistake, and he owes money on the car. So he trades it again, hoping, each time, that this time the promise will be true, that the car will make him happy. But it only impoverishes his wallet along with his spirit.

The farmers bought machines for the same reasons. How little many of them were needed can be seen in a drive along back roads in that part of the country. They sit alongside barns, or in sheds, and once in a while in a little park of their own, half a dozen of them in a group, abandoned and rusting. A little work and oil and paint and they would perform their function as well as ever; they would cut the wheat or pick the corn. But they are no longer needed to do it. The men who bought them have left the farm or sold it; they have moved their labor to a factory, and if they live on the farm at all, they may not work the fields or even walk them on Saturdays, save perhaps with a dog and a gun, hunting for pheasants and rabbits.

The machines were a promise, and they kept it only to themselves. They did not give us a better life on the land, only a way to show ourselves that our individual labors, the small farms we wanted so badly, were no longer economic. For most farmers in Mecosta County, the frantic cycle of bigger, easier, better, newer, more costly machines has ended. Those who are still earning a living from the land have big tractors and matching equipment. Elsewhere, the machines sit idle, rusting, not mothballed like the World War II ships in the California harbors, but just as obsolete, and no one pretends that they will be needed again. The investments have been written off, the bills paid, and the machines are content to rust away. They do not wish to work, as a man or a horse might. They have no desire to breed and produce milk again, as a cow might if she were turned away from the dairy. The machines are creations of man, not nature, and they do not need us any longer.

The chemical warfare goes on. For a few seasons, we used the miracle spray DDT like the Salk vaccine. It killed the flies, cleansed the fields of bugs. But the immunity increased, and bigger and bigger doses were needed. Finally, the state outlawed DDT, before all the birds died and the fish were all killed in the streams.

We are captives of our technology. We need more fertilizer to grow the big crops that the machines need to make themselves profitable. We concentrate so many cattle in a small space that their manure becomes a disposal problem rather than a valuable by-product as a natural fertilizer.

For most of the land, however, peace has returned. In fifty years, we went from a time when the church bells rang across the parish, and the horses and men could hear them above the noise they made, to a time when the tractors drowned out everything and a man had to have a wrist watch, dustproof, to tell him when to break for dinner. The potato fields, where young people once called across the crates, became the province of the noisy, impersonal harvesters, and no voices were heard. But we cheated too much, and now no noises at all are heard in those fields. The children have gone to the cities, to play basketball on the asphalt. The men have gone to the factories and the shops and the offices. Many of the fields are abandoned, and nature has taken them back. Little trees are growing up around the barns and the stone piles, and here and there in the fields. The creatures that waited so patiently in the fence rows have hopped and crawled out again and begun to multiply and reclaim the fields. They outlast the machinery in the long run.

In some of the fields I tilled as a youth, the natural growth has come back so strongly that it is becoming difficult to remember that men had fully claimed the land from nature. Lanes that cows kept cropped are growing up to pin cherry trees and scrub bushes. The old cow paths have been plowed up and are gone. The grass has nearly overgrown the foundation of the windmill, and the barn doors are rotting.

Nature is a fussy old librarian, and she wants all the books in place, left untouched, only dusted now and again. She does not want to share her bounty with man. She wants the land for herself and she will have it. It is difficult to believe, here and there, that we were more than an interlude, suffered patiently enough by nature who knew that she would have things her own way in the end. And perhaps she will. Perhaps the farmer, like the warrior, never wins the final battle.

10. THE WAR AND ITS AFTERMATH

For us on the farm, unfeeling or unthinking as it may seem, World War II was a time of optimism, and buoyancy, long days of enthusiasm, a time of last promises.

For one thing, we felt that it marked the end of the depression, that persistent albatross that dragged its dreary weight behind us all those years, making the steps less light and the hopes more empty. My father remembered the

(175)

days of World War I, and the stories his father told of them—soaring prices for wheat and potatoes, boom times, high demand for everything, rush in and win, pay the farmer, make him rich too, for once, not just the munitions maker and the profiteer. It is impossible to know how they weighed on my parents' spirits, those long miserable depressed years of the 1930s, when, time and again, things did not work out. We children never knew, and they have forgotten, how many bills were never paid, how many plans were put off again and again until finally they were quietly given up and not spoken of any more, little dreams of the future bartered away for the sake of sane survival.

How many hand-me-down clothes did they accept for their children? One of my father's sisters married a streetcar driver, and by comparison with ours, their family seemed loaded with worldly goods. How many times were they unable to give their children something they really wanted—a ride on a merry-go-round, a bottle of pop, an ice-cream cone, a firecracker? My father had developed a bitterness about it all, and it is difficult to fault him for it. He had done what he had been expected to do—he had married; he had sired children and had them baptized; he had gone to church regularly and obeyed the commandments; he had bought a farm and stocked it and put out crops and harvested and met his commitments to the bank and to his friends, and he had helped his neighbors and taken in passers-by when they needed aid.

And what had he got? The potatoes had not made him rich, or even retired the mortgage; the cattle had become diseased, prices had gone down, not up, and the odds never broke for him. The children had been ill, and no one can ever know how humiliating it is for a strong, independent man, proud and ready to work hard, to have to negotiate with a hospital about bills he has no way of paying, bills he incurred to save the lives of his children.

He had worked hard; God, he had worked hard. He had run the thresher, he had hired out by the day, he had worked by hand when he could not afford to repair broken machinery. The horses had not always been able to cope with the hard clay. When it had turned up rough and lumpy, too coarse for planting, he had gone out with a wooden mallet and walked around on the knoll behind the windmill, breaking up the clods, hoping to subdue the earth by his own muscle when the strength of the horses and their machinery had not been enough. Once when I was small and knew nothing of these particular agonies, I ran up behind the barn to bring him home to supper and found him sitting on a clod of clay, mallet handle between his knees, face in hands, sobbing softly to himself, defeated, humiliated by the nature he had believed himself to be in partnership with. I had the child's wisdom to know that this was not a time to help, so I waited until he seemed to have settled his spirit a little, and then I ran to him as a child will. He threw me up on his strong steaming shoulders and carried me to the house, tossing the mallet in the tool shed as we came by, and I held on to his hair and his forehead, drinking in the rich smell of my father, smell of earth and sweat and cattle and straw hat and work, and I knew the world was in place.

But naturally buoyant though he was, he came to blame

others for his failure. He had done what he should; it had not worked; someone must be at fault. The bitterness would take a new edge later but it had begun to shape itself by the end of the 1930s, and it would have been harsher had he not had the church and the family to help. Elsewhere, it led the farmers of America to the edge of revolt; near Remus, it led my father only to the threshold of despair.

And now perhaps it was over. Butter prices went up, the Guernsey herd was flourishing, and perhaps we would have money at last. One good crop of potatoes, one healthy harvest of wheat, and if all should come in the same year, the mortgage would vanish forever and the dream would come true after all.

As for the war itself, we must be forgiven for not taking it very personally. My father had not been beyond upper New York State in any travels; he had no real knowledge of the German land where his parents had their roots. They had fled to a new land where dreams beckoned, and they did not nourish their children in love for the fatherland. America was their country, Germany a place where the dream had failed.

We had no reason to believe that our place was threatened. We had hardly heard of Japan, and never of Pearl Harbor, but we knew, as we sat by the old Atwater-Kent radio that day, that we were at war. We were immediately gullible to the most clumsy propaganda, and we prepared for the war as a high-school football player prepares for a game. There was no room in our minds ever to consider defeat; we would win—and perhaps prosper in the process.

We were putty in the hands of the publicists. We believed the comic books and the movies, and that it was only a matter of time before simple good triumphed.

Clouds gathered, but we brushed them away. The Office of Price Administration was created to prevent excessive inflation; as it turned out, it kept us from getting rich. We did not know that it would not prevent those already wealthy from advancing their fortunes still further. We still thought we were capitalists; populism had not captured us. There was gasoline rationing, with A and B and C stickers, and my father was personally offended because a neighbor got a B sticker while he got only a C. But we still lived with the clumsy bureaucracy; it would all work out somehow.

We patched up the old Ford car, a bastard model, that 1937 60. It never really worked, body or running gear, but we could live with it. We put boots in the tires and patches on the tubes and kept it rolling. Top legal speed was 35 miles an hour, so a little bounce in the wheels was all right. Now and then, we couldn't get new tires and, for the wagon, were driven to filling the old ones with beans when there were no tubes left that would hold air. In short, if there were material deprivations, they were nothing new, and now there was reason for them.

The young men went off, one by one, until the big flag in the church had more than a hundred blue stars. Mothers put the little flags in their windows, blue for a boy in service, gold if the boy was killed. All through the long war years, we prayed each Sunday that the parish would have no gold stars. A cousin of mine was captured, but, at last, they all came back. You see, we told ourselves, we are doing the right thing—the dream will come true after all.

My father, born in 1904, was too young for the first war and too old for the second. My oldest brother was just too young; our family was intact, the war did not threaten. And there was the air of urgency, of new opportunities. Men were away, and their farms had to be worked. There was money to pay help; my oldest brother made a few dollars in that kind of work, and a few more in black-market trading of gasoline stamps.

It would be only a little time now, my father could see —the war meant money, and the mortgage would be retired. His sons were old enough to help, indeed old enough virtually to take over with just a little guidance and decision-making from him, and he would not be alone. The word "alone" took on greater importance in his conversation. He would not have to work the fields alone, do the chores alone, prepare a grist alone, cut the grain alone. His boys were growing up. Soon, now, we would be ready to paint L. Stadtfeld & Sons on the barn.

Some prices rose. Wheat sold higher, so did butter. And the need for hired labor made a change in methods that was more important than we realized at the time. My father bought a small grain combine. It was a Case, with a 4-foot-wide sickle bar, powered by the tractor. It cost perhaps $400, and he more than paid for it the first year, cutting grain for other farmers at $3.50 an acre. The second year, it paid for the tractor and finally made a contribution to retiring the mortgage from the farm. It marked the first move at our farm toward this kind of mechanization. We saw it as a convenience, as a generator of cash. In a short time, there would be combines all over the area and the opportunities for custom work would be much less. The combines got bigger and more efficient, and relatively cheaper. The availability of good used machines hacked away at the custom market, and there was a passion to own your own equipment. Dad later owned a larger combine, but it never made him money the way that first one did. But, more importantly, it was a breakthrough for mechanization.

The excitement of the war brought us all together. Families planned excitedly for the day when the boys would come home. They shared the V-mail letters, and there were the times; always somehow unexpected, when a soldier on leave would arrive in the night to stay for a few days, fine in his smartly pressed uniform, shiny shoes, and ribbons. The soldiers talked a new language, talked of the places they had been and the beer they had drunk, and they were men, owning an experience their fathers could neither share nor interpret, suddenly secure in their own personal patch of past where they knew more than any who stayed behind.

We should have known, and perhaps the wiser parents like old Otto did, that they would not come back and take up the old life they had gone off to protect. They had swaggered down the streets of Frisco and Paris, got drunk in beer halls on godforsaken islands that none of us had ever heard of. They had shipped out from Pearl; they had stormed up the sands of Iwo and Tarawa and the Canal. They knew about the Solomons and the Mariannas, and they had odd souvenirs picked off dead Japs and Germans. They had killed men, and they had seen men die next to them and been glad it had not been they. They had seen things they would not talk about, things they did not want to think about again forever.

They had driven jeeps and halftracks and thrown them away in an orgy of carelessness that made them forever impatient with frugality, forever disdainful of thrift. They had seen bulldozers tear down forests and jungles and build whole airfields overnight, and they would never have the patience to use a horse-drawn stump puller. They had seen things bigger than their fathers ever imagined—cities, oceans, ships, trucks, tractors; they had ridden in huge airplanes. They had done big things, and they had built up a passion for action that would drive them, once they got rid of the nightmares, to try to do big things again on those farms that had been, in size and ambition, always small.

We were ready for them, we thought, ready for the boys and the boom times. The mortgages had been paid off, though the farmers were far from wealthy. The earnings of the older members of the family had helped out; the future seemed clear. The buildings had been painted, except for the barns, and everybody was ready for the postwar boom.

When they first came back, the boys were simply weary. We had waited with such impatience that it took time to adjust to the notion that they did not share that eagerness, at least at first. They wanted to rest.

Our neighbor Otto had always been up to milk by 6 o'clock, and his son, home from the horrors, wanted to sleep until noon. The hell with the Jerseys; they had got themselves milked while he was out saving the world, and they could damned well get themselves milked in the same way now for a while.

We put a cot in our dining room, and the boys would come by and nap there, long deep sleeps haunted a little with recent memories. But the nightmares faded away, and in a little while, they did not need to slip over to our house to sleep.

We had acquired a sort of pool table, a coin-operated affair discarded from my maternal grandfather's restaurant, which we installed in the basement. A bare bulb hung above it, and everyone came to use it. On Sunday the yard would look like a used-car lot, with five, ten, fifteen cars scattered around and perhaps twice that many young men drinking their beer and whooping and yelling around the pool table.

Nothing was done to the basement; I can still smell the potatoes today, although that may be imagination. The walls are the old stone of the foundation, the ceiling the rafters, no windows, a concrete floor. But the boys had seen many worse places, and no one cared how loud they yelled, no one counted their beers, and there were no air-raid sirens.

After a little while, they turned to work. Suddenly, surprisingly, as though no one had counted before, it became apparent that there were more boys than farms. Almost immediately after that, they began to realize that with the new tractors, and a milking machine, a fellow could run the home place and a neighbor's, too.

But more than that, they discovered that there was money in the factories, turning out automobiles and refrigerators and all the other things that had been postponed for the duration. A chap could go to a factory and with nothing but his hands and the willingness to endure unpleasant conditions—no more unpleasant, really, than the worst days and the worst jobs on the farm—could bring home $80, $100 a week. There was simply not that kind of money on the farm.

And there were things to buy with it. First, there were the cars that had survived the war. Old Fords and Chevys and Plymouths, sometimes with the running boards all rusted away and replaced with elm planks; sometimes cars already nearly twenty years old, nursed tenderly by the young vets because a guy who had torn all over Europe in a jeep had to have his own car, after all.

Radios, too, and clothing—everybody needed a new set of civvies—and watches and cameras for those who had not brought them back from abroad. They bought a lot of playing cards, too. In the old days, we had a family deck of cards, and every year or so, when it got so sticky we could hardly use it, we would put a pile of talcum powder on the dining-room table oilcloth and rub the cards around in it, shaking off the excess after they were coated. They would be slippery again for weeks. But the boys had no such patience. They snapped the decks like professionals, which many of them were close to being. They broke the corners and they threw away the old decks and bought new ones. They threw away a lot of things that were old, and bought new. They had learned about that in the army. Ash-can it.

Such ideas had no roots in Remus. We had saved, conserved, been thrifty, made do, made things last. But all at once we were ready to consume, to throw out the tablecloth when it began to fray and get a new one, to trade the car, swap the tractor, buy bigger and brighter farm machinery.

The war changed us from savers to consumers. There was a rush, all over the nation, to junk the old things and replace them with new. We bought with a pent-up fury, fueled with cash saved in the war. Factories rushed to respond to those desires, and the country filled up with the good and the bad, the decent and the ugly. We put glass blocks in the houses we built, not because they did much either functionally or artistically, but because somebody offered them for sale. We went from wooden chairs and tables in the kitchen to furniture with legs covered with chromium and seats covered with plastic. Cars began to run to gadgetry, first because the people would buy anything, no matter what amount of extra-cost junk was on it, and then because somehow we had fallen into the habit.

We are beginning to recoil from that a little, the pendulum swinging back as it always does, and our wives haunt the antique shops and roam the country roads, paying out our good money for the things we threw away a few years ago.

Few of the other values prevailed, either; the system simply blew apart. There was more explosive force to the war than what was dropped on Berlin and Tokyo and Hiroshima. There was a social explosion, and it lasted longer and had more dramatic impact than the bombs.

The old system was based, not only on thrift, but on isolation. Things had been happening in our own country, let alone in the world, that we knew nothing about. If there were mansions in Newport and, closer to home, in Charlevoix and Petosky, we really were not aware of them or that they meant that we were by comparison poor. But now the boys knew. They had buddies all over, from all kinds of places and lives, and the country could hide fewer of its secrets. Even the church began to bend a little, for the men had seen the big cathedrals and in some cases had shot other men in them or dropped bombs at them. The sanctuary did not seem quite so sacred to them.

They all smoked cigarettes, because there was no time for the pipes their fathers had smoked. Ready-mades. In the war, we had bought little rolling machines and made cigarettes. But the boys had bought them for almost nothing, and their habit was formed. And they had the money to buy them by the pack.

They married girls from distant places. Cars had made them mobile, and they went to see buddies who, it often turned out, had sisters, and families states apart were joined. City girls came to live in the country, or vice versa, and the cash system of the city, with the conveniences and the shelves of knickknacks, won out in both cases.

There was the GI bill, and it paid for some schooling. In our area, few used it to go to college. Some learned typewriter repair and things like that, but more spent the money on short courses in agriculture from Michigan State. Of course they were compelled to use what they had learned and to use it immediately. Old methods were junked peremptorily, and their fathers, who had often only vague notions about why they did certain things a certain way, had no defense against this onslaught of new ways.

The horses had to go. A few oldtimers clung to their horses as a child clings to his teddy bear, or an old man in a rest home to a favorite walking stick though he may not walk out any more. But the time for horses was short, and in less than a decade, there was not a real working team in the area.

This meant that much of the machinery had to be replaced. We had horse-drawn mowers, for instance, and it was difficult to slow the tractor to the pace. We cut the long tongues short and put metal straps at the end with holes so they could be hitched to the tractor drawbar, but the tractor was restless, and it made the man pulling the machine impatient for something faster. This had nothing to do with a need for something faster; it was a desire forced on us by the capacity of the machines, not by the need to speed up the work.

Take the hay mower as an example. The old horse-drawn model, converted to use by the tractor, could cut a couple of acres an hour. The mounted mowers, geared for the tractors, could do three or four times as much. But it might take an hour, or a half-hour, to mount the mower. And if you had a 10-acre field to mow, it was a difference of four or five hours of work versus two or three. That is not enough difference to merit the price of a new mower.

But machinery has an integrity of sorts. It seems strange to pull an old mower with a shiny new tractor. Perhaps it interferes with the picture we have of ourselves and the mechanical extensions of our lives. It makes more psychological sense to have a fast tractor hitched to a fast mower, so we fill in the picture, even though it might be more economical to blur it a little. We bought the fast mounted mowers if we could possibly afford them, just as old Otto built the stile in the fence, to fill in the picture. The old men shook their heads, but there was nothing to do but step aside.

Of course the cycle of the new machinery fed on itself. Once you had the faster mower, you found yourself bottlenecked by the old hay loader, for there was no point of laying down more hay than could be brought to the barn in a day of work. But the fast mower had intruded itself; it led to the purchase of the baler, where a gang of men and later on a man alone could package his entire hay crop in a day or two. The logic was relentless. The hay crop could be expanded to make use of the ability of the machinery. This meant more acres, either bought or rented from an older farmer ready to stop working, and with his sons gone away to the city.

But what to do with the hay? More cattle, the milking

machines, more crops, which meant bigger machinery, more powerful tractors, a whole cycle. While this was pushing us into a money economy, prices stayed the same. Figures cited by the *Michigan Agriculture Statistics* bulletins make the point clearly enough. In the years 1950–54, farmers received an average of 41 cents a dozen for eggs. In 1968, they were paid an average of 33 cents a dozen; in the fall of 1971, the farmer received about 30 cents a dozen for medium-sized eggs, slightly more for large ones. The average price to the farmer for hogs in 1950–54 was $19.96 per hundred pounds; in 1968, the average price was $19.00 and in the fall of 1971 they were a bit over $20.

All beef cattle sold by farmers in Michigan in the 1950–54 years averaged $20.44 a hundred pounds. The average 1968 price was $19.00. Farmers were paid an average of $2.22 for a hundred pounds of potatoes in the 1950–54 period. The 1968 price was $2.13, and, interestingly, the average price in the years 1915–1919 was $2.18.

The price to the farmer for whole milk has risen, largely as a result of dairy associations which function much like unions. Thirty years ago, farmers were being paid $1.73 for a hundred pounds of milk. In the years 1950–54, the price had gone up to $4.05; in 1968, it was $5.51. The average price is higher now; in the Detroit milkshed, it runs around $6.00 a hundred pounds for Grade A milk, the kind sold by the quart and half-gallon in stores for about 25 cents a quart. The retail price is about double the amount paid to the farmer, the markup going to the bottlers and stores.

It is little wonder that, since 1953, the number of farms in Michigan has decreased from 146,000 to about 85,000, the total number of acres in Michigan farms from more than 17 million acres to less than 13 million. If the rate of decrease in farm land were to continue at the same rate, in about fifty years there would be no Michigan land in farms. This is an improbable statistic, but one that alarms nonetheless.

If you like to be frightened by statistics, consider that in 1939 Michigan farmers used about 144,000 tons of commercial chemical fertilizer on about 18 million acres of farm land. In 1968 they used 828,899 tons on 13 million acres, an increase in the range of eight times.

And so the mechanical tiger, loosened by the war, slowly devoured the little farms. The old ways would no longer serve, and the new ways led to a treadmill which many eventually abandoned voluntarily or were forced from.

It was a sad thing to watch, that casual destruction of a way of life. The dreams held by generations were destroyed, and the tragedy was compounded because the destruction was so casual, almost unconscious, like a parent's simply not noticing that his child's toy is broken and not making any attempt to repair it.

Elsewhere, edges of the old ways still persist. In the cornbelt, and in more fertile parts of Michigan, where the land lends itself to cultivation in big parcels by large machinery, or where specialties are possible, there are still farms, and men draw their livings from them. Some of them are even "family farms," owned by a family and operated largely by it. But more of the big producers are run by corporations, with higher skills in balancing the books for accountants.

In the corners of my own county, men still persist in some of the old ways. A man who once prided himself on his butchering skill, and who was noted as the best sausage maker in the parish, still rises early to go down to the barn, though his old hands can no longer milk a cow. Another man, his wife gone, sits alone in the big house in the winter, hearing the echoes of the children and friends and family that once filled the big rooms to bursting, all scattered now to new places, to towns new since the war, to little houses with color television sets.

And the sound of crickets is much louder in the summer evenings than it has been for a long time.

The agricultural economists in the university smile and say that this is simply progress, that the American way is to be efficient and the new big corporate farms are more efficient, and they have coined the term "agra-business" to show how they prepare young men from the farm country to earn salaries in the city.

They say, too, that the farmers of today are richer, better off. They have far more money than their fathers did, and if there are fewer of them, so be it.

And they are right. Food is relatively cheap in the city, though there are markups necessary on converting it from the raw product of the land to the thinned-out, packaged and boxed, self-preserving product the housewife picks up in the supermarket. It is my fault that I remember so well. Perhaps the milk was not so much better, the frozen vegetables may be almost as tasty, the packaged potatoes will probably not poison my children. But the bread has no character. The margarine is not beaded with moisture the way the butter was when we brought a new chunk up from the cellar. I do not know the name of the cow it came from; in fact it came from a soybean plant. The bond between us is gone.

But still we were no harder on the land than the Indians were, and it would have lasted us forever. We cared more for the cattle, and every stalk of corn, every square of land, meant something. A man who has grown his own crops and bred his own cattle is no candidate for the Skinner Box.

And are their dreams so much better, those young men, now graying, who left the farms and went to the city? They despair of their children, who seek out escapes that can often be fatal. And the young people dream of something else, something real. Their fathers do not pray for rain but thank God it's Friday, in a wretched admission that the week is just barely endurable. They hope they can make it to retirement in good health—"30 and out"— so they can exchange the wretched empty years for some peace, perhaps on a little place in the country or by a lake where they can fish as their fathers did, or have a little garden by the trailer in Florida.

It is true, of course, that the farms were hell on women. But that need not be so today, because the medical care they so desperately needed could be brought in, the dreary parts of the isolation are ended by the mails and by the electronic communications equipment, the horrid drudgery of the kitchen eased by modern conveniences.

Not all men want to farm, but not all men want to be sculptors, either. It would be nice to keep the choice more open.

The war—"our" war, World War II—opened up the back country of America, made it aware that there was a whole big world out there where people had more things, where everybody seemed to be having a lot more fun, where the work wasn't so hard, where there was more money. And it brought the machines to the farm, making it possible for one man to grow more and more crops, selling them at the same price, still making a living, but still not making much more. The result is that prices of raw food products have gone steadily down relative to the price of everything else. A great market has opened up for intermediate steps in food processing and handling, and these cost more than the raw food.

The way the old way of life came to an end is probably not all that different, really, from the way it came to an end in some countries when they were "opened up" by the "advanced" nations. It is a continuation of a process begun when the Spaniards began to civilize the Indians of South America, when the traders and farmers and miners needed protection from the Indians as we civilized, developed, opened up the West.

But the real question is, have we improved the human

condition? Is man in the factory better off than man on the farm? More broadly, is man in the city better off, happier, than man on the land?

If not, then it has not been progress. Nor is it any longer an answer to say that only an industrial society can provide for the great numbers of people. Unless we are prepared to say that we are really no more advanced than the lemmings, that we must resort to war and famine and pestilence to control our population level, and that if the atomic war comes it is too bad but inevitable, that we are not ready to do anything basic about the conditions in which we live, then we must consider alternatives.

We should know that once, in the farm country, a system worked, and people were happy. There really should be a way to keep what was good, to add things that really represent progress, and not destroy the fabric of life along the way. We are beginning to see that we must live with our planet, and we must live with ourselves, too.

EPILOGUE

High in the limbs of a hard maple tree, high as blind rage can drive a boy to climb in flight, high enough to shut out the shouts of pursuing parents and other unwanted company, the evidence still stands. A quarter century of new growth and twenty-five hard Michigan winters have not obscured it. I carved the words up there with a sharp jackknife, and I carved them deep to match my rage. I put them there because I knew that I could safely share my hurt with the tree, that it would shade me from rebuttal and discussion while I put down my record of rebellion in tall letters—carving words because that made more sense than whittling. The words do not express my feelings today, but they did then: "I HATE MUSIC, MOSTLY PIANO." I never told my mother that I had put them there, but she knew I had run out of the house and that the piano-lesson days were over. Perhaps she thought that day that she had lost the struggle to civilize me, to gentle me, to open me up to things not of the farm. In fact, though, my revolt left me free to go the other way, all the way to the center of the farm life, and to find there a little emptiness that made me turn from it to something else.

The experiment with the piano had begun promisingly enough. I had learned to read early, and I was an obedient child. My hands were long and deft; I could reach a full octave. Our old piano, a relic with the player mechanism torn out, had been salvaged from a fire where it had been declared a total loss. We picked it up free and used it some thirty years. My older sisters took lessons on it. We scrounged the practice books, chickens paid for the lessons, and I learned quickly. By the time I climbed the maple tree, I could pick my way through sheet music. But I had been pushed into the classics too soon, and I had no foundation for them. Popular music I could hear on the radio, but there was no place for me to hear Bach.

Also I sensed, not able to put the feeling into words but with the knowledge deep inside me, that the piano lessons were not part of the enterprise in which we were involved as a family—the enterprise of the farm. Had my father encouraged me, or if the family had taken some pleasure in sitting around the piano in the evening as one or another of us played, music might have meant more. As it was, the piano stood between me and the farm, and I had to oust the intruder. No one thought to tell me that my friends would grow up and go away and we would no longer play in the woods together, that fields might grow over and barns might fall in on themselves, but that the music would be with me for the rest of my life. Or perhaps they did, and I simply did not listen.

In any case, I stopped the lessons and went out to the land, but the outside world won out after all.

A sick cow marked the beginning of the end. One of our Guernseys came down with something. I do not remember what; she may have picked up a nail or contracted some disease worse than we could cope with using the little tubes of penicillin or some other antibiotic that were abundant and cheap after the war. She was a good cow, a regular producer, calf every year, perhaps 400 pounds of butterfat every gestation, docile and durable. And suddenly she was sick and might die, and we called the veterinarian.

The real vet. There was another man in the community who had had some training long ago, and Dad sometimes called him when the cows needed more help than we could give. Whenever he was called, I railed at my father. The man didn't know his medicine. He didn't wash his boots before and after going into the barn, he had only a dim memory of some long-past training, and I never trusted him. He could clean a cow, but there might be parts of the placenta remaining, or he might not have sterile gloves and so might infect the cow himself. I hated to see him come on the farm. But he worked cheap, his animal care a sideline to help support his tired farm.

This cow deserved the good vet. He came and tested and prescribed with some degree of confidence. Standing by his little truck afterward, we talked while he scrubbed his boots. What did I plan to do after high school? Farm, of course—was there anything else? What about being a vet?

It was a sunburst in my brain. Somehow it had never really occurred to me before that I would not stay on the farm, following in my father's footsteps, doing better, making a better living, but repeating his successes, avoiding his mistakes, going on, putting myself into the picture in which I had grown up. My sons are already wondering about what to do with their lives. They have only a little understanding of what I do and so are not drawn automatically to it. They have to think, but I did not. And suddenly thought was thrust at me.

Of course I could be a vet. I could make money helping take care of others' livestock. I could have a nice truck, recent model, one that would start in the winter and be warm inside. And another car at home for my pretty wife to drive around town. A farm, of course, with all the solid life that goes with it, but also the money from a practice.

Did I have the brains? Of course. Did I have the money for college? No, but that was no problem. Could I get in? Well, why not?

So I checked with the school principal, who was delighted that someone was thinking about college. I read the Michigan State catalog front to back; upped my study time to an hour a day, so that I would get all As and Bs. Wrote to State, sent in transcripts and letters, received an entrance scholarship that would pay my tuition.

One day I told my father that I was going to go to college. He grunted and we went out to make a grist. I was a little offended at the time. Though we had gone through a difficult period as I struggled into adolescence, high anger between us often, little if any communication save on his terms, still, I thought, shouldn't he be pleased for me?

It would be years before I had any intimation of the wrench that my announcement must have caused him. My oldest brother was gone by then, working in a factory, coming home on weekends with long stories of the beer he had drunk with his friends, working on his car, working also on getting the wildness out of him that grew as he left the dull farm and moved to the city where there were money and a new life and always things to do. My other brother was in the service, a peacetime soldier, somehow intellectual, and although his love for the land seemed more than mine, he had decided long before that he would not have the money to take a farm, that farming had moved away from him and he would not be able to come back to it. My oldest sister was married to a man for whom the land had no lure, a factory worker who had no interest in the farm. So suddenly, the realization was forced on my father that the cycle would end with him. He would be left alone with no one to help, he would farm out his years, and then it would be over, the plans at an end and no name painted on the barn.

And I suppose I had looked so promising. I had bought

registered cattle—Jerseys; he would have preferred more Guernseys, but I had come under the influence of a large Jersey breeder and that seemed the way to go. I must have had half a dozen head by the time I was a senior in high school. I bought registered Duroc-Jersey hogs, too, lovely slim red things, the sows littering under heat lamps, the beginning of a promising herd.

I had been an officer in the local chapter of the Future Farmers of America—though never president. But I had medals enough to cover half the breast of the blue-and-gold jacket, medals for public speaking and good projects, and finally a gold medal as a State Farmer, one of the young men who was making a name for himself. My scramble calf had won second prize at the fair, and all the guys I ran around with were planning careers on the farm —when they could scrape together a few bucks.

I had read all the books in the ag library at the high school and knew the lineage of half the registered dairy herds in the country. If I could have had a trip of my choice, it would have been to Vermont to see some of the famous old Jersey herds there, to talk with the herdsmen I had read about in *Hoard's Dairyman*.

Now and again, I even did things for which my father could praise me. I was careful with the tractor, plowed and cultivated with caution and concern. I could pull a cross-cut saw, run the combine, do anything that needed to be done. One winter, while my father was working away for the only time in his life to pick up money to pay some debts, I had made an experiment—I had milked three times a day and proved that the production would go up.

EPILOGUE

True, I also read Shakespeare, but only to show off really, to impress the English teacher or a girl. As it turned out, the teacher was impressed and the girl was put off, a lesson which escaped me.

But my father had every right to expect me to stay. I had never planned anything else. And now there was to be this parting, this new start for me, this ending for him. If he wished, privately, that I would fail and come home, it would not surprise me.

I am sure my mother was secretly pleased, for the life had been hard for her, and she hoped for more for us. She helped me to shop for towels and socks, put my name on them. My cattle were not discussed; I was to leave them there, for I might be back.

Graduation time, commencement, the parties, the last summer. Hard work, the last really steady full physical exertion of my life. Plus a part-time job, found for me by the vet, testing cows, from which I made several hundred dollars, so that when I left in the fall I had cash enough to carry me through half the year.

The last days. Plant and harvest until time to leave. The hay and grain got in, but I would miss silo filling. I snuck old shoes into my pack and would keep them with me to help against the home sickness which washed over me in waves. Saying good-by to the cattle, the last milking. My oldest sister and her husband were to take me to my dormitory; on a Sunday morning we left for Lansing, not quite a hundred miles but some light-years away.

I nearly dropped out a dozen times. The shock was almost too great. But, somehow, once I had started, I could never go back. There was nothing to do but press on, change my life all the way, make a new life, adjust to new things.

And yet all the words I ever carved in the maple tree down the lane were still there. My feet still walked the paths to the woods and my pitchfork still hung between two nails on the center post in the barn.

Like tens of thousands of other farm boys in those years, I left not in anger, not in retreat, but in search of new promise. My parents, and theirs, could not know that we could never really go away, never push from our lives those rich years on the farm.

None of us can forget the cows, the crops, the fields, the fences, the heartache and the wonderful promise. We remember forever that we were once a part of something whole; we struggle to make our children part of our world in the same way, but we do not succeed, because that life was too full, the sharing too close and too simple, to duplicate now. Always our heads turn when we see a tractor in the fields. If the grain is waving in the breeze, we check to see if it is ready to harvest. We applaud straight rows, scoff at scrub cattle or a badly cared-for set of buildings.

We did not deceive our parents or our pasts; the times did, and we were captives of the times, as captive as our parents were. We saw new sounds and heard new lures, sought new places and found new lives. But we never really left, and the soil is still in our souls.

ABOUT THE AUTHOR

CURTIS K. STADTFELD was born on the family farm in Remus, Michigan, in 1935 and received his B.A. in journalism from Michigan State University. He was employed by several newspapers in Michigan and received his M.A. from Eastern Michigan University, Ypsilanti, in 1970. At present, he is Director of Information Services and Assistant Professor of English at Eastern Michigan University. Mr. Stadtfeld lives in Ypsilanti with his wife Jacqueline and sons Peter and Christopher. This is his first book.

ABOUT THE ILLUSTRATOR

FRANKLIN McMAHON is an artist and writer with studios in Lake Forest, Illinois. His drawings, paintings, and reports on events of social and political significance have been published by almost every U.S. national magazine. He is the recipient of the Renaissance Prize of the Art Institute of Chicago and was named Artist of the Year by the Artists Guild of New York. Mr. McMahon visited Remus and the Stadtfeld farm in order that his drawings might be authentic illustrations of places mentioned in *From the Land and Back*.